Polling
Green

E. D. MARCU

Abaris Books, Inc. New York

SIXTEENTH
CENTURY
NATIONALISM

For Monique

CONTENTS

Lansquenet Drummer, woodcut by Hans Wandereisen,
circa 1550.

Introduction

And why should not... twilight be recognized as a useful reality as well as the sharper rays of high-noon?

Charles E. Merriam,
Political Power

We should not ask too much of definitions; ideas might best be understood approximately.[1] Nor should we ask too much of dates; many and conflicting answers have been given to such questions as when a concept was born, or when it acquired the meaning we give it today. History leaves behind too much, or too little. In the first case, the historian has the difficult task of selecting and rejecting evidence in order to understand and explicate the past. In the second case, he is forced to assume the priest's role, as he interprets fragments, signs, tokens.[2] We have been living with both difficulties—arbitrariness and exegesis—for a long time, but the dangers from either side are fortunately attenuated by new findings and constant reversals of judgment. Then also, special interrogations of narrow aspects, of details that are lost in larger treatments, have often been the means of breathing new life into seemingly dead arguments, of shattering fixed opinions. With this in mind, I would like to raise the question again of whether or not there existed a genuine national consciousness in sixteenth-century Europe.

The choice of the sixteenth century imposed itself on me, as I encountered, almost incidentally, so much chauvinism in the period that I wondered about modern critics who had decided that those expressions of pride for country, people, and king did not constitute nationalism of a kind we meet with centuries later. It seemed worth looking into the problem. The six countries chosen—Portugal, Spain, Italy, Germany, France, and England—represent an interesting cross section: Catholics and Protestants, small and large, insular and continental, early centralized and not at all. Together they form a wide arch across Europe, from southwest to northwest; the two not-yet unified countries framed on either side by two that had accomplished a fairly complete consolidation.

While the words—and the ideas—"nation," "nationality," and "nationalism" are not new, attempts to assess them are rather modern. Efforts at definitions and at dating have been so numerous that the divergency of opinions has here been brought together in two lists, one containing proposed definitions, the other dates advanced for the emergence of the proper kind of national feeling. The lists, appended to this Introduction, do not presume to be complete, only varied enough to make the point, namely that nothing is firmly established, that there is room for discussion.

In histories of nationalism, it is generally held that the Ancients cannot be credited with a sense of nationality: the Greeks because they were parochially preoccupied with their home cities; the Romans because they were saddled with various, faraway possessions. They were too internationally minded as a people. The Europe of the Middle Ages is also said to have provided the wrong soil in view of the period's bent for universal, that is, cosmopolitan, ideas. As to the "Renaissance,"[3] some critics have felt here an embryonic sense of nationality, one reason being that humanists echoed classical concepts.[4] For such traces, scholars seem to prefer the term "patriotism," although this word presents as many problems of definition as "nationalism."[5] Apparently, not before the second half of the eighteenth century—and most dramatically, during the French Revolution—were the masses of Europe finally roused to the appropriate state of patriotic passion.

However, a number of thoughtful studies have seen this question too in a different light. Nationalism is believed to have existed at all times, everywhere, now stronger, now weaker. One author, for example, who had set out to search for traces of national consciousness in the truly medieval period between the eighth and the thirteenth centuries, could not detect any difference between the attitudes and emotions of medieval and modern man as regards people and fatherland.[6] Another investigation into the problem concludes with this conviction:

> Nationalism is not the product of an age, class, party, religion or philosophy, but...each has partly contributed to its growth, partly counteracted it.... Germs of nationalism are latent in all strata of society, and when a great crisis arises, the national passion may break forth with a power which nobody would have foreseen.[7]

And it was Meinecke who has shown how nationalism sometimes arises in contact with, and in opposition to, universal ideas.[8] Contradictory concepts do coexist in society. Special interest groups will frequently, perhaps honestly, proclaim their love for their native land, all the while pursuing their own aims: religious or political dissidents will seek help from their country's enemies, as will merchants try to maintain trade with them.

In contrast to some authors, who have simply asserted that it is anachronistic to speak of nationalism in the sixteenth century,[9] Federico Chabod at least has substantiated his opinion with telling arguments.[10] He too thought that whatever it was that stirred in sixteenth-century man's heart, it was not nationalism of the kind we find in the late eighteenth and in the nineteenth centuries. We might therefore look for a moment at the period that ostensibly seems to many to represent a fully evolved and, most importantly, a mass-supported nationalism.

The French Revolution, again and again regarded as the curtain raiser for nation-states and national sentiment, did neither break out over a nationalistic principle, nor did it liberate or create a single nation. Its program appealed to mankind at large: "patriotism became identified with respect for the Rights of Man. The true patriot was a citizen of the world."[11] In fact, people streamed into France from all parts of Europe to support and propagate the revolutionary ideas. Some historians discover acute nationalism only in the wake of the revolutionary enthusiasm.[12] And if we take into account the opinions of the last generation of French historians, the case for national fervor of a new quality becomes very weak indeed. Not one of them has been impressed by any nationalistic element in the outbreak of 1789.[13] On the other hand, no new spirit was necessary for the ensuing years of liberation, for the fighting and dying of attacked or occupied countries all over Europe: the call to defend territorial and spiritual possessions has been obeyed from Salamis to Stalingrad. Nor have all historians discovered evidence of mass support in the nineteenth century. It has been argued that then nationalism was strictly the concern of the elite, while "for the masses in general the test of nationality was still religion.... The very fact that nationalism was represented by middle class and gentry was enough to make the poor suspicious."[14] The two latecomers to unification and independence, Italy and Germany, took their time until the last third of the nineteenth century. Throughout the eighteenth century, Germany's finest minds were very little attracted by the idea of political unity.[15] It was by the reluctant nationalist Bismark that the country was finally led into nationhood. To judge from complaints years after the establishment of the nation-state, the masses were in no way aroused by the innovation.[16] Even among university students, the old particularism was apparently stronger than any eagerness to go to the barricades for a united fatherland.[17] Italy, for her part, did not bring off her independence without foreign, that is, French, help, nor without paying for it with portions of her territory. Here, too, the lower classes were hardly drawn into the liberation movement.[18] Elsewhere, we find that Poland underwent one more partition, and that Greece, just liberated from a foreign master, offered her throne to several foreign princes. And finally, with the autocratic wind blowing through Europe after decades of violence, many idealistic patriots had to leave their homelands in search of safety and service abroad. New forces, entirely unrelated to national passions, had moved to the center of attention: industrialization, scientific discoveries, accelerated colonialism, and, in addition, socialism and communism, with their divergent ideals of class consciousness (that is, favoring one sector of the nation) and international brotherhood (that is, reaching out beyond one nation-state). One wonders, given these conditions, why historians attribute to the nineteenth century a degree of loyalty to land, ruler, fellow countryman that they deny to the sixteenth. Why, indeed, should the nineteenth century, as filled with revolts and revolutions as the sixteenth, have presented itself as the propitious moment for nationalism? It seems rather that every period embraces elements militating against an ideal moment of national feeling, because at all times religion, politics, or economic interests will contend for the good patriot's soul and will carry off important parts of it.[19]

What had more likely changed in the intervening 300 years was the mode of dealing with the impulse to love the homeland above all others rather than any quality or quantity of the impulse itself. Concepts like nation, state, nationality, nationalism, patriotism were now studied in the same scientific way that was applied to fairytales as well as to bacteria. Old structures for thought, old subject matters, old vocabularies had been discarded. Abandoned were mirrors of princes, moral treatises on rights and duties of rulers and subjects, and the traditional ties between politics and religion.[20] Repeatedly treated in the nineteenth century, the question of nationalism was taken up in our own age with new intensity, impelled, perhaps, by the breakup of political conglomerates after the First World War, and more vigorously still after the Second. More and more states were created and needed theoretical and emotional justifications. Communism, like its ecumenical predecessor, Catholicism, could deflect national emotions only briefly. Communism, on the contrary, incites and supports national tendencies in emerging nations, for political reasons. Nationalism after the last war has clearly become an exasperating problem for ever growing numbers of uprooted individuals and groups faced with the personal and bureaucratic question of where they belong.

For my part, I shall be satisfied to define a nation as an association of people that has outgrown the tribal stage, and whose members call themselves, and are called by others, Poles or Chinese, Germans or Englishmen.[21] By then, they would have acquired a sense of belonging to something sufficiently unified and recognizable as to offer a comforting extension of individual customs; customs differing from those of outsiders and which, for some reason, always seem to be the better customs. Nationalism must be one element of man's competitiveness and combativeness, of his need for something familiar in a mass of unsettling human and nonhuman events, and most certainly, too, part of his capacity for loyalty and self-sacrifice in causes that often elude his grasp and competence. It might be part of our organizational disposition of body and mind. We automatically simplify complexities in order to comprehend them, as we—automatically, it would appear—differentiate mankind according to size, color, sex, age, profession, language, and origin. We distinguish between those who resemble us and those who do not: the outsiders, the foreigners. Since we might be dealing here with elemental realities, possibly the very structure of the brain, there is, of course, little room for moral judgments in a search for national manifestations.

As we investigate different countries with their differing developments during the course of a hundred years, we discover that both hope and despair, both longing for greatness not yet achieved and nostalgia for greatness remembered, arouse passions identically expressed. Everywhere we find the same xenophobia and boastfulness, which in erudite hands might flow into history writing and genealogical investigation, supporting, "scientifically," equal claims of superiority.

To these unruly notions we must add the relationship between ruler and people. Whether ecclesiastical or secular, hereditary or elected, authoritarian or institutionally checked, whether admirable or despicable, the ruler and his office benefit from the irrational awe that attends power. A monarch can count upon a good deal of leniency from his subjects: as he represents them in a heightened capacity, they are willing to defend him and the common land.

Nationalism is not here assumed to have been a central concern to sixteenth-century thinking. But, as I attempted to show, it cannot be said to have been central to the nineteenth century either. There are probably no themes that are central to any period, except during moments of crisis and even then not all sectors of a population are equally affected.

One aspect of national consciousness in the sixteenth century was the tug-of-war between the vernaculars and Latin, a struggle that went on amidst wars for land, influence, and religion. The battle for the mother tongue was only partly won, and we will, in each country, keep track of its progress.

The texts examined are not exhaustive, if for no better reason than that they cannot be exhausted. To offer a great variety of voices seemed sufficient to demonstrate no more, no less, than that nationalism in the sixteenth century was noisy, fanciful, and plainly fashionable. Dressed in its contemporary style, with its contemporary vocabulary and associations, it was neither quantitatively nor qualitatively different from later configurations.*

---

* All quotations appear in English. Where I found no translation, I have translated the text myself.

Definitions of Nationalism*

1920   G. P. Gooch, *Preface of Nationalism:* "Nationalism is the self-consciousness of a nation, and its flowing current is fed by many streams. The nation is an organization, a spiritual energy.† All attempts to penetrate its secret... break down before the test of experience."

1923   R. Johannet, *Le Principe des nationalités,* p. 15: "National sentiment is rarely distinguishable from patriotism.... We may say that it is a patriotism based on the awareness of belonging to a same origin, or having the same deep interests as other inhabitants of the same soil."

1924   M. Vaussard, *Enquête sur le nationalisme,* p. 1: "Deceptive word—full of diverse meanings!"

1926   C. J. Hayes, *Preface of Evolution of Modern Nationalism,* p. 61: "Nationalism is plural rather than a singular. [It is] the paramount devotion of human beings to fairly large nationalities and the conscious founding of a political 'nation' on linguistic and cultural nationality." The author has tried more than once to come to grips with the slippery concept, the last time being in his *Nationalism: A Religion* (1960) p. 2: where he says; Nationalism "may best be understood... as a fusion of patriotism with a consciousness of nationality."

1926   L. Romier, *Nation et civilisation,* p. 69: "Elementary nationalism is nothing if not a passionate form of political materialism.... Nothing agrees better with the concept of civilization than love of fatherland,... one of the essential forces of civilization."

1927   F. Meinecke, *Weltbürgertum und Nationalgeist,* pp. 12-14: "It is a consciousness that begins in an impersonal, a slumbering, vegetative manner, which, when its time has come, develops into a conscious will of nationhood."

1929   W. Mitscherlich, *Nationalismus,* p. 3: "Nationalism is one of the most powerful forces dominating our present public life... one of the most complex phenomena of a centuries-old social, cultural, political, and phenomenal evolution."

1934   J. Huizinga, *Im Bann der Geschichte,* p. 134: National consciousness as well as patriotism are "eternal instincts of human cohabitation."

1937   F. Hertz, *Nationalgeist und Politik,* p. 11: "Nationalism is to be understood as a nation's consciousness of its power and its prestige. All other values... are subordinated to it."

---

* Related concepts (or terms), such as nation, nationality, patriotism, present the same difficulties, the same vagueness, the same contradictions.

† The "spiritual," "emotional" explanation seems to stem from Renan's answer to his own question "Qu'est-ce qu'une nation?" in his lecture of 1882. Yet Saint-Juste had already written: "The fatherland is not the soil, it is the community of affections." Note found after his death. See Ollivier 1954, p. 233.

1946-47   H. Koht, "The Dawn of Nationalism," p. 265: Nationalism, like other concepts, underwent many changes of meaning, "perhaps even more than others because it is just as much a psychological as a political term."

1952   H. Rothfels, "Grundsätzliches zum Problem der Nationalität," p. 342. The author quotes G. B. Shaw to the effect that a healthy nation does not feel its nationality any more than a healthy body feels its bones. Rothfels adds, "Opposition and suppression provoke a conscious and emotional condition that drives men far beyond [Meinecke's] vegetative level of nationality."

1953   K. W. Deutsch, *Nationalism and Social Communication.* This work is an attempt to master the problem with the help of the tools of modern sociology, i.e., with graphs, statistics, and mathematics. On page 144 we find this definition: "National consciousness is a feed-back of secondary symbols in an information-processing system." And p. 155: "Nationalism has...appeared as...a dominant power...[which] like a whirlpool [is the] visible expression of the meeting of other forces which created it."

1956   H. L. Koppelmann, *Nation, Sprache und Nationalismus,* pp. 12 ff. National feeling is a matter of habit. It rests on fiction promoted by slogans. It is a mass emotion of which masses are unaware. While not a natural phenomenon, it develops easily under certain conditions.

1963   Meyers Neues Lexikon, entry entitled "Nationalismus und Kosmopolitismus." The encyclopedia was published in the German Democratic Republic. The term nationalism is judged according to whether it occurs in "oppressed" countries, where it is justified, or in "exploiting" nations where it is defined as reactionary, middle-class, instigating hostility, and deflecting oppressed nations or classes from the class struggle.

1966   G. Ritter, *Das deutsche Problem,* p. 55: "Nationalism is extreme and biased consciousness raised to the point of arrogance."

1967   E. Lemberg, *Nationalismus.* The author knows his problem too well to attempt an overall definition, rather his aim is to describe different models of nationalism at different places and times.

Here follow a few more titles that avoid definitions while demonstrating the potency of the idea:

1967   H. Seton-Watson, "Nationalism and Imperialism," deals with the wholly unresolved question of nationalism in the Soviet Union.

1968   L. Snyder, *The New Nationalism,* pp. 5 ff.: "There is no such thing as a new nationalism," except that the idea has spread to the awakening nations in Africa and Asia. The complex situation in the Soviet Union is described beginning on p. 290.

1971   E. Allworth, in *Nationalities in the Soviet East,* provides a list of publications in U. S. libraries. The introduction gives a brief survey of the ideological dilemma of the Russian leaders, from Lenin on, in the

12

treatment of autonomous aspirations of the various nationalities in the *U.S.S.R.*

1971 *Soviet Nationality Problems,* a collection of essays concerned with the unresolved problem of nationalism at home and abroad.

1971   A.D. Smith, *Theories of Nationalism,* p. 4: "The main focus of this work is sociological: the relation of nationalism to economic development and social and cultural modernisation, in the conviction... that nationalism is deeply embedded in this wider trend."

When Did Nationalism Begin?

1874   T. Mommsen, *Römische Geschichte,* vol. 2, pp. 412 ff. The celebrated historian of Rome, himself a German nationalist, leaves no doubt as to Rome's national consciousness. He points to such special Roman qualities as state-forming and state-conservation; her assimilatory, unifying, legislatorial, administrative, in a word, civilizatory, gifts: not to mention her patriotic literature and art.

1905   B. Monod, *Le Moine Guibert et son temps,* p. 235: The fourth chapter of the book, entitled "The Awakening of National Feeling in Eleventh-Century France," describes Guibert of Nogent as a consciously patriotic Frenchman. On pages 236 and 237, the author invokes the *chansons de geste* as proof that France was at the time already "a nation in the modern sense of the word."

1913   W.S. Ferguson, *Greek Imperialism,* p. 114: Although the Greeks never did achieve unity, calls for it were common, as common as the presumption that Hellenes in general belonged at the head of the honor roll of nations. See also Plato, *Republic* 469-471.

1916   H. Finke, *Weltimperialismus... im späteren Mittelalter,* p. 39: The Sicilian Vespers and the Bohemian revolts of the thirteenth century are examples of early national emotions.

1916   E. L. Woodward, in *Christianity and Nationalism in the Later Roman Empire,* develops the thesis that nationalism expressed itself all over the Christianized Roman world in the form of heresies, as anti-Roman actions in religious guises.

1923   R. Johannet, *Le Principe des nationalitiés,* p. 18:"As far back as the twelfth and thirteenth centuries, national feeling appears in a pure state, distinct from loyalty toward the king, as the flower of carefully reflected patriotism."

1927   G. Grosjean, *Le Sentiment national dans la Guerre de Cent Ans,* pp. 213 ff: The Hundred Years War saw, at its conclusion, the "definite victory of the feeling of national unity in France."

1927   F. Meinecke, *Weltbürgertum und Nationalgeist,* p. 12: The will to become a nation first seized the French, then, in the nineteenth century, moved on to Germans and Italians.

1928   T. Walek-Czarnecki, "Le facteur national dans l'histoire ancienne," pp. 559-61. The author believes—despite some hesitation—that the role of nationalism in the history of every people is so important that its existence in antiquity cannot be doubted.

1931   C. Hayes, *Historical Evolution of Modern Nationalism,* pp. 291-93. There was no striving for political unity and independence prior to the eighteenth century. "Universal mass-nationalism is peculiar to modern times." The author finds, nonetheless, strong national consciousness in England before the eighteenth century.

1931   K. G. Hugelmann, "Das deutsche Nationalbewusstsein... im Mittelalter," p. 4. National consciousness is not a modern phenomenon: it already existed in the Middle Ages.

1933   E. Hettich, *A Study in Ancient Nationalism.* The author's thesis that a strong national consciousness existed in ancient Greece is supported by copious quotations from Greek literature.

1934   J. Boulenger, "Le vrai siècle de la Renaissance," p. 30. It was in the twelfth century that national sentiment, at least in France, was "reborn."

1934   J. Huizinga, *Im Bann der Geschichte,* p. 138: "In the land of the Franks we suddenly hear the fanfare sound of a totally new national consciousness," a jubilation mixing Christianism with a primitive, barbaric arrogance, as evidenced in the proud Prologue to the *Lex salica.* On page 139: "European nationalism has begun its march across history." The Prologue dates from the eighth century.

1935-37   G. G. Coulton, "Nationalism in the Middle Ages." The essay is a thorough indictment of Christian xenophobia and narrow nationalism during the crusades—in the Church, in the monastery, in the university— consistently supported by popes and emperors.

1936   H. Mombauer, "Bismarck's Realpolitik als Ausdruck seiner Weltanschauung," pp. 75-76. The French Revolution had awakened political awareness, and "raised political thinking to a national experience... [which] ignited... irrational nationalistic passions."

1937   A. Choulguine, *Les Origines de l'esprit national moderne et Jean-Jacques Rousseau,* p. 16. France had achieved the state of national unity before other countries, "but as a mass, she had taken consciousness of herself only after or during the great Revolution."

1938   B. C. Shafer, "Bourgeois Nationalism in the Pamphlets on the Eve of the Revolution," p. 50. Nationalism, cumulative like all movements, "had accelerated on the eve of the Revolution."

1938   G. Weill, Forword to *L'Europe du XIXe siècle et l'idée de nationalité.* In the nineteenth century something new arose in Europe: "the general awakening of national preoccupations."

1939   W. Goetz, *Das Werden des italienischen Nationalgefühls,* p. 53: "No state in the West had acquired [national] feelings before the thirteenth century."

14

1939   H. Kohn, "The Nature of Nationalism," p. 1001: "Nationalism as we understand it is not older than the second half of the eighteenth century.... Its first great manifestation was the French Revolution."

1939   R. Syme, *The Roman Revolution,* p. 440: "Out of the War of Actium [31 *BC*].... arose a ... myth, which enhanced the sentiment of Roman nationalism to a formidable and even grotesque intensity."

1940   G. Dupont-Ferrier, in "Le Sens des mots *Patria* et *Patrie* en France au moyen âge...," pp. 92 ff, finds early use of the word "fatherland" precisely congruent with present usage.

1940   M. Bloch, *Feudal Society,* p. 432. The thin stratum of educated men, the clergy, had no national concept, while we have no evidence of what the masses thought. "In order to discover the obscure foreshadowings of nationalism we must turn to groups of men more simple-minded and more prone to live in the present... to the knightly classes and that half-educated section of the clergy which confined itself... to reflecting... the public opinion of the time."

1941   V. H. Galbraith, "Nationality and Language in Medieval England," p. 117: "The sentiment of nationality is... a continuous thread in the stuff of English history, present in some primitive form from the beginning."

1943   E. Ph. Goldschmidt, "Medieval Texts and Their First Appearance in Print," p. 70: "It is in the latter part of the fifteenth century that the concept of nationhood and national consciousness began to spread in Europe."

1946-47   H. Koht, "The Dawn of Nationalism in Europe," p. 266: The twelfth century "saw the first expressions of European nationalism. It is a remarkable fact... that a truly national consciousness, though limited in its scope, burst forth almost simultaneously in many of the European countries."

1948   P. Courcelle, in *Histoire littéraire des grandes invasions germaniques,* pp. 12, 13, 207 ff., stresses the pressure of the barbarian invasions, which aroused patriotic fervor among pagan as well as Christian Romans.

1952   A. Toynbee, ed., *Greek Historical Thought.* The historians referred too often to achievements common to all Hellenes not to have had a clear consciousness of their national character. See, in particular, pages 54, 60, 75, 117, 162-63, 182, 199 ff.

1955   H. Kohn, *Nationalism,* p. 9: "It was not until the end of the eighteenth century that nationalism in the modern sense of the word became a generally recognized sentiment, increasingly molding all public and private life." On page 10: "As a rule, wars before the French Revolution did not arouse deep national emotions."

1955   B. C. Shafer, *Nationalism: Myth and Reality,* p. 5: "Any use of the word nationalism to describe historical happenings before the eighteenth century is probably anachronistic."

1956 V. Ilardi, " 'Italianità' among some Italian Intellectuals. . ." p. 340: "Nationalism is of recent origin. It dates from the era of the French Revolution."

1956 H. L. Koppelmann, *Nation, Sprache und Nationalismus.* The author is very skeptical about the whole idea of nationalism, suspecting that it was probably no more than an illusion or a delusion. Yet he thinks that the eighteenth century offered the most encouraging circumstances for its growth and that the French Revolution gave it a last and lasting impulse (pp. 196-210).

1959 H. Mitteis, *Staat des hohen Mittelalters,* p. 98. English national feelings are awakened by the Norman invasion. On page 181: In Spain, the reconquest could rely on a national spirit already evidenced in the seventh century; on page 187: opposition between nations surfaced dramatically among the crusaders.

1961 J. P. Seguin, *L'Information en France.* The study shows the pervasive chauvinism in early gazettes. Two poems written in 1498 exalt national unity under Louis XII (p. 45).

1966 G. Ritter, *Das deutsche Problem,* p. 55. The vague consciousness of national particularity became a mass phenomenon only with the French Revolution and its mass politization.

1967 F. Paschoud, *Roma Aeterna,* p. 18: The Roman world became acutely aware of its oneness at the time of its absorption by non-Roman peoples. On page 329: The idea of Eternal Rome was the last weapon of patriotic Romans.

1968 L. Snyder, *The New Nationalism.* According to the author, there is no such thing as new nationalism. On page 6: National tendencies were accentuated by the English, the American, and the French Revolutions. Patriotism thereafter became the glorious banner "under which men gave their lives to achieve or maintain nationhood."

1969 D. Douglas, *The Norman Achievement,* p. 33. Despite general absence of national sentiments in the eleventh century, there were representative individuals in eleventh-century England who "seem to have been conscious of an overriding English unity which sectional interests should not be allowed to disturb or destroy."

1971 J. Godechot, in "Nation, Patrie . . . en France au XVIIIe siècle," p. 501, has fixed the date for genuine nationalism, at least for France, around 1840.

1975 O. Ranum, ed., *National Consciousness, History, and Political Culture in Early-Modern Europe.* This work contains six essays by six authors on six European countries in the early modern period. Each piece goes its own intellectual's way but remains uncertain about the basic problem of national consciousness and any precise date for its maturity.

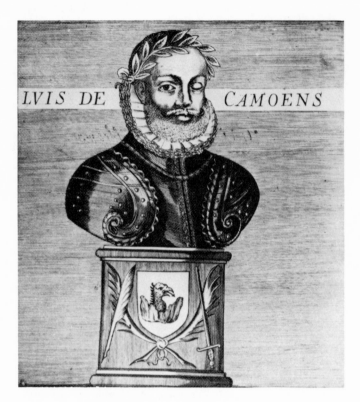

Portrait of Luis de Camoes, engraving.

Portugal

All by itself this little country would prove the case for national consciousness in the sixteenth century; it could even prove a case of special national obstinacy.[1] Seamlessly bound to a larger country, Portugal refused to accept the logical consequence and become a Spanish province. Like a closed fist, it undertook its short and adventurous world role, conquering, discovering, overextending itself, losing its strength in the process, and, finally, following a series of internal difficulties, falling victim to the waiting neighbor. But Portugal suffered the indignities of Spanish occupation for no more than sixty years before regaining its freedom, and, without reclaiming any special importance within Europe, has remained independent since. Despite all theories, its history also informs us that the lower classes were most fiercely involved in the fight for freedom before and after the Spanish takeover of 1580.

When Charles V, emperor and king of Spain, retired to Yuste in 1556, leaving the kingdom to his son Philip II, he had not lost his interest in political affairs. In 1557, he sent emissaries to Portugal with the mission to influence the court in favor of a succession to the Portuguese throne that would bring the country under Spanish command. The emissaries' reports were discouraging. They disclosed that in one way or another, the people were so opposed to a foreign king that no one could predict accurately what they might do to subvert such an outcome.[2] We read how the Portuguese Cortes dealt with national problems during the minority of King Sebastian: in the winter of 1562-1563, the Cortes imposed on the regents

17

not only strict military orders to keep the country intact but also directions for the young king's upbringing. Sebastian was to be instructed to eat like a Portuguese, speak Portuguese, act like a Portuguese, and dress in the Portuguese manner, so that he would learn to love his kingdom.[3] Eighteen years later, Spain under Philip was still trying to incorporate Portugal. Meanwhile, in 1578, Sebastian had undertaken a senseless campaign in Africa, losing the battle of Alcázarquivir and his life in an unnecessary show of heroism.[4]

The defeat was catastrophic for the country, and it opened the way for Spain. The painful process has been minutely described,[5] the descriptions revealing that the people, that is, the representatives of the third estate, were alone in holding out against foreign rule at the Cortes of 1580. The clergy had long been won over by Sebastian's successor, the old king-cardinal, Henry, and the nobility, tempted by Spanish promises and money, had given in too. Only the "commoners, undeterred, declared their readiness to die rather than obey Philip."[6] The speeches of their leader Febo Monis, his reported discussions with the old king, and his intrepid resistance were certainly comparable to examples from antique literature, or, for that matter, to any nineteenth-century national-minded oratory.[7] The country, however, had neither money nor enough leaders to support its brave representatives.

Portugal was taken over by Spain, and the helpless rage of the population found an outlet in the messianic fantasy that King Sebastian was not dead (in fact, his body had not been found on the battlefield), and that he had retired to a monastery and would soon come back to free his people.[8] The sixty Spanish years witnessed the appearance of four false Sebastians, who, thanks to Spanish vigilance, had no more than short-lived successes. The glorification of an inglorious king, seen by his people as an incarnation of old Portuguese virtues, gives some idea of their despair and also of the extent of their participation in national affairs. We cannot overlook this when we try to evaluate earlier national emotions.

Shortly before unfortunate Sebastian died, the no less

unfortunate wanderer and poet Camoẽs returned to Lisbon after seventeen years in the distant parts of the Portuguese empire. Aware of the country's decline, and, as if to exorcise inexorable fate, he had written an epic of and for his people, *The Lusiads*. Every commentator has stressed the national intention and effect of the poem, its praise of the handful of brave men from one of the smallest countries of Europe who had achieved what the vaunted greater nations had become too decadent even to contemplate: the opening of seaways, the bringing of religion to savages and riches to Europe. The resemblance to ancient Rome was not neglected in the poem, for it lay not only in the Portuguese language, "barely corrupted" from what it had been during the Roman Empire, but also in the country's talent for empire-building. Or, as Camoẽs says: "Destiny's intention was to make humanity forget Assyrians, Persians, Greeks, and Romans" (1. 14). Every biographer has quoted the moving words from a letter that Camoẽs wrote shortly before his death: "And so I come to the end of my life, and all will see that I loved my nation so well that I was content to die not only in it but with it."[9] Camoẽs' epic summarizes and symbolizes the ambition of a people who had come to believe themselves to be God's elect.[10] By the end of Camoẽs' life, this belief might have been shaken, but the brief and astonishing past was to sustain the Portuguese for centuries to come.

The vernacular was propagated everywhere, here as elsewhere in Europe. We might just be lacking sufficient contradictory material, but it would appear that the claim for the mother tongue never became immoderately strident in Portugal: possibly because the energies of the country were absorbed in the task of holding its possessions together and of keeping its people free of Spain. Portuguese was evidently used early and unselfconsciously, if a well-born and well-educated cosmopolitan like Damião de Gois, diplomate and friend of Erasmus, learned Latin only in his late twenties and while he was abroad.[11] (He was a fervent spokesman for his country's achievements, and he defended, in particular, Portugal's imposition of monopolies, an example of national selfishness furiously attacked by Portugal's commercial rivals, only to be imitated eventually by all of them).[12] If the national language had a rival, it was Castilian rather than the humanists' Latin.[13] A cultivated author knew, of course, what he owed to the classical texts, and what quotations were expected by his learned colleagues. Yet the Portuguese claimed for their idiom the greatest similarity to Latin of all daughter-languages, and taking the argument a step further, declared that in modern times it had surpassed Latin in all branches of literature.[14] As for Castilian, they asserted its inferiority to Portuguese in both content and euphony.[15] Grammarians, poets, and humanists mixed praise of their mother tongue with political and imperialistic expressions, in a word, with nationalistic ambitions. The language was to be used as a weapon in the hands of the conquerors.[19] As one critic formulated it, use and care of the vernacular in times of strength are the prerogatives of the powerful, while, in times of sorrow, such use and care become a duty for those who will see to the preservation and unity of the nation.[17] Indeed, pride and despair are the twin themes in the tale of the language's defenders.[18]

Pride, despair, claims to divine election, comparison with Rome and, alternatively, with the glorious past, appeals to countrymen to attain the virtues of their forefathers: all this we will find, in turn, in the other countries.

Portrait of Philip II, engraving by H. Wierix.

Spain

It would be a happy discovery that enabled us one day to disentangle human motives, to determine their sincerity and the relative importance of their components. How, for instance, did Ferdinand and Isabella, the "Catholic Kings" par excellence, reconcile their filial obedience to Rome with their managerial skill and sense of national responsibility when they informed the pope that he was not to meddle in Spanish affairs?[1] After Isabella's death, Ferdinand enhanced his international standing even more and further developed the conviction that he alone was to rule the country, and that meant including Church-related matters.[2] Machiavelli, for one, had no doubt that Ferdinand used religion to advance his political aims.[3] Again, how did his heir, Charles V, accommodate his undisputed piety when he decided that the pope of his day deserved a lesson and so did nothing to prevent the sack of Rome of 1527? When Alfonso de Valdés, the Erasmian, and secretary of the Emperor, wrote an apology for the pillage, what were the elements of his motivation in exculpating Charles and attributing all the blame to a sinful papacy?[4] As we read his version of the events, we wonder why Rome was not sacked more often, and whether at some point Valdés would have objected. Under the expert rule of the next king, Philip II, no Spaniard had to fear any royal weakness in dealing with eternal threats to the country's preeminence in matters political or religious. Pope Sixtus V saw the king's religiosity as a pretence, believing that "his principal aim was the security and aggrandizement of his dominions."[5]

In the successive courts of sixteenth-century Spain,

then, we find strong emphasis on political, that is, national, interests. But the lower classes, too, expressed intense desire for "Spanishness" in the administration of their country. When Charles I—not yet elected emperor as Charles V—arrived in Spain and presented himself, in 1518, to the Cortes at Valladolid, the third estate submitted a long list of grievances and requests. Points five to eight of the list insisted that offices, benefices, dignities, and provincial governments should not be accorded to foreigners; that the King give no "nationality" to foreigners, or, had it already been granted, to revoke it; that ambassadors of the realm were to be Spaniards; that servants of the palace were also to be Spaniards; that it might please the king to master the Spanish language soon, so that he could better understand his vassals and they him.[6] Charles spoke mostly French, and the request that a king speak his people's language seems natural. It is, however, noteworthy that the third estate had requested it. Two years later, in Toledo, the King was again asked by the third estate not to give offices to non-Spaniards. Charles, now emperor, was preparing to leave Spain for Germany. The estates, unable to prevail upon him to remain in the country, insisted that he not bring back foreigners in his service but use *naturales.*[7]

Good rulers are expected to have no other aims than to unify and to defend their lands. We think it normal for subjects, proud of their monarch's achievement, or anticipating deeds to come, to transfer local patriotism to a greater unit, to the whole country, or, in Spain's case, even to a world-wide empire. Court historians tend to praise the hands that feed them, their monarchs' as well as the country that has produced such an eminent line.

We might mention here a Sepúlveda, who, as royal historian, wrote a strictly Spanish-centered history.[8] The case of another historian, the Jesuit Mariana, is, however, different. Both Mariana and Sepúlveda have made names for themselves in other fields: Sepúlveda through his participation in the discussion about whether the American Indians were by nature slaves, and Mariana by his recommendation of tyrannicide.

Mariana had authored a thirty-volume history of Spain in Latin; then, discovering to his dismay that Spain had no history in the vernacular, he translated the work himself, his intention being to give the people a sense of their national existence and of their past. In the prologue to the Spanish version, he explains that when abroad he had often been asked about the origin of the Spanish people and their greatness.[9] Thus, Mariana's history—not a court history—is imbued with a sense of nationalism.[10]

But, then, in the domains of politics, diplomacy, or historiography, expressions of allegiance, exclusiveness, pride, and self-interest come naturally, It is odder to find outright chauvinism in the ranks of the clergy, particularly in the Spanish branch of the Jesuit Order. The Company's twentieth-century historian, Astraín, himself a Jesuit, has tried to explain the origin of this mentality.[11] He believes that an "excessive Spaniolism" pervaded the Court and infected the Jesuit Order just as it infected so much of the remaining Spanish people. In Spain, everything, including religious matters, was to be decided without resort to Rome. Spaniards were convinced of the superiority of their brand of Catholicism. They were Catholics par excellence: their kings were *Catholic Kings,* their victories *Catholic victories.* Another reason for the Spanish Jesuits' prejudice was, Astrain thinks, their conviction that the Roman Court was the center of moral turpitude.[12] We may, however, doubt this latter point when we remember that, only a few years earlier, the founder of the Society had laid the bodies and souls of its members at the feet of the papacy. In fact, Astraín goes on to say, in the second half of the century much was improved at the center of Christianity. We are left, then, with the persuasion of an unequalled Spanish faith, a faith which, as we shall hear, feared contamination as much through the agency of nonnative Catholics as from Prot-estants or Turks.

The disturbance inside the Company that Astraín goes so far as to call "schismatic," had apparently begun around the person of Loyola's nephew, Antonio Aroaz, Provincial Father of Castile.[13] Aroaz had manifested a certain rebelliousness even while Loyola lived, and his opposition found a focus when Laínez was elected to the generalship of the Order following its founder's death. Laínez had been among Loyola's first coworkers, but the fact that he was a "New Christian," a convert, was hard for the group around Aroaz to bear. Even after the death of Aroaz, it was in these circles that opposition to Rome was prevalent. They insistently demanded that the General of the Order be a Spaniard and live in Spain, independent of Rome, "to avoid the danger of heresy." A Spaniard living abroad should not be allowed to function as general, commissary, or visitant. Customs differing so greatly from country to country, they should not be mixed. Another perceived threat was that monks traveling between Rome and Spain might be used as spies, and, in any event, would take too much money out of the country.[14] The esprit de corps clearly ran along national lines.

The finest flower of national exclusiveness, however, was the Iberian preoccupation with the purity of their citizens' blood. At first no more than a device to establish a Spaniard's religious standing, after centuries of neglect of racial questions, the pure-blood concern seemed to have flowed imperceptibly into all arteries of the country's life. It became a mental and moral burden, and, with the investigation of so many cases— the prerequisite to filling positions on the basis of ancestry—it created as well an ever-tightening bottleneck.[15] Under pressure from all sides, the Jesuits finally renounced the well-known views of their "Saint Patriarch"[16] on that score and decided, at their General Congregation of 1592-1593, no longer to admit New Christians. Here their historian stresses once more the close relationship between Loyola and Laínez, whose ancestry had made Aroaz and his friends so uneasy.[17] In this context, we hear again of the Jesuit Mariana. He wanted nothing to do with the absurd concept of pure blood, believing it to be rarely found in contemporary Spain. Yet he made common cause with the Jesuit dissenters in thinking that Spaniards, having founded the Order and raised it to its present eminence, should not take orders from abroad or from foreigners, and he too opposed electing non-Spaniards to the generalship.[18]

Pure blood, nevertheless, had become the guarantee of orthodoxy, of nobility, of the Spanish sense of honor.[19] The country, says one author, had dreamed itself into the role of the elect of God.[20] A biblical ancestor, Tubal, was discovered;[21] books and treatises informed the Spaniards that Spanish law had preceded Mosaic law by 600 years or that Spaniards were heirs to Israel's mission on earth, except that they had surpassed Israel by bringing to a new world the word of God.[22] Apparently, the country firmly supported the claims of eminence and exclusivity. A modern historian of the Jesuits, Boehmer, sees in the Society's deviation from the convictions of its lawgiver an urge toward "Spain for Spaniards."[23] Kamen, another historian of our time who studied the Spanish Inquisition, underlines the popularity of this institution,[24] as Bataillon had done before him.[25] And it is Sicroff's thesis that the search for pure, or rather for impure, blood became a national frenzy.

The Spanish language, meanwhile, was not being neglected. Like the other vernaculars, the language of the Spanish people needed the help of the learned in order to become respectable. Throughout the century and beyond, formal defenses of the vernacular followed one after another, and their authors were not merely grammarians, but also Spain's philosophers, theologians, orators, and poets.[26] In 1492, Nebrija had dedicated his Spanish Grammar to Queen Isabella with an important program note as introduction.[27] Political power and language, it said, were companions; they begin, flourish, and decay together.[28] Since the Spanish realm was now secure, the time had come for the arts. He had always wanted to contribute something to Spain's greatness and so offered this grammar, a regulation and fixation of the still-lawless mother tongue. Without such codification, the language would become incomprehensible to future generations. The historians' encomiums about rulers and their deeds might be lost to posterity, but with a regulated language, royal immortality was assured.[29] Here as elsewhere in Europe, the propagation of the vernacular was mainly, though not exclusively, in the hands of humanists, that is, of professional Latinists. And so the criticism of Latin, the desire to equal, to surpass, and even, in some cases, to obliterate it, had to play itself out in the hearts of the Latinists themselves. Habits, cultural vanities, fashions, and convictions worked their manifold pressures upon the authors.[30]

The patriotic note is sounded in the very title of a two-volume anthology of some hundred poets of the period.[31] For us, the most celebrated writer in the collection is Cervantes. While we find no noisy "Spaniolism" in his prose works, he did express the imperialistic ideas of his countrymen in his poetry—though perhaps only at certain moments of his life. There are, among other pieces of Cervantes, two *canciones* in this anthology, collectively called *A la Armada invencible*.[32] In the first, written when rumors were circulating to the effect that the Spanish fleet was having difficulties at sea, he voices his hope for success, praising the righteous cause and its heroic defenders.

The second *canción* takes into account the naval defeat, which the poet attributes to natural causes, regrets that God willed it so (at least for the present), and exhorts the country to close ranks in expectation of future victories: "O Spain, O King, O Famous Soldiers," he ends the second poem, "propose, command, obey so that Heaven must finally help your just zeal...!" In a similar vein, Cervantes wrote a long dramatic composition, *El Trato de Argel,* describing the miserable life of Christians living in Algiers under Moorish domination and imploring the king to liberate the city.[33] And again, in a letter to the king's secretary, he expressed his hope of Spanish intervention. Here Cervantes' motives were more personal, as he himself was then a Christian prisoner in Moorish hands.[34]

Nationalism is not a likely cause for mystics,[35] nor, at the other extreme, for authors of picaresque novels. But patriotic fervor is much in the foreground in the abundant literature of historic or pseudohistoric epics and romances of the sixteenth century. It was an ideal arena for accounts of Spanish bravery in the face of Moors, Turks, or American Indians.[36] The old Ronceval tale was taken up once again. Contemporary writers were apparently inspired by Ariosto's *Orlando Furioso* (published in 1516), although it was now treated from a Spanish angle.[37] A native hero, Bernardo del Carpio, invented by "patriotic passion" in the twelfth century, now accomplishes Roland's adventures and is the victor at Ronceval.[38] The intention was to obliterate the Italo-French tradition, but the Spanish version was by chance also somewhat closer to the historical truth than the *Chanson de Roland* and its progeny. Commenting on the enduring popularity of the heroic narratives, George Ticknor says that, in nearly every one of them, there lives "a proud patriotism which is just as presumptuous and exclusive under the weakest of the Philips as it was when Charles V wore half the crowns of Europe."[39]

It would seem that the sixteenth century had little if anything to learn from the Romantic Age in the way of flamboyance of national pride.[40]

Portrait of Nicolo Machiavelli, woodcut, c. 1550.

Italy

Guicciardini once asked himself whether Italy would have benefited from a monarchic government. His answer was negative, because then her cities might never have developed their greatness and diversity.[1] This was no more than a theoretical consideration though, for, like his fellow Italians, he deplored the national disunity; but it was an alternative to the constant reproofs of princes and institutions for immorality and decadence. Yet why Italy, of all countries, was unable to generate a dominant center is, like Germany's similar fate, an historical enigma.

By the sixteenth century, many countries, even the vast territories of Russia, were well along on the road to centralization. Under the same sky, on the same soil, ancient Rome had achieved a cohesion and coordinated energy, which her descendents, declaring themselves the legitimate and only heirs, did not allow to be forgotten. Throughout the middle ages, never did Italy relinquish its claim of succession to the old world center. If Dante's call for a revived imperium was its literary expression, Cola di Rienzo's fourteenth-century extravaganzas were among the attempts to transform fantasy into reality.[2] Injured pride and desperate hope may have led a L. Valla to confuse past and present when he proclaimed that "we continue to hold sway in much of the world by this other power [the Latin language]: Italy is ours, Gaul, Spain, Germany, Pannonia, Dalmatia, Illyria, and many other peoples," because, he continued, and still using the present tense, "the Roman empire is where the Roman language rules."[3] Florence was proud of having been founded by Rome,[4]

29

Milan wanted to be a second Rome,[5] Venice was declared a happier, saner Rome,[6] and Viterbo had local "documents" forged to prove that it's past was even more cultured than Rome's.[7] Literati, historians, and philosophers immersed themselves in the style, rhetoric, manners, and mannerisms of the exemplary Roman past, a past all their own until the lofty dream had seized the rest of Europe as well.

Why did this cultural uniqueness not lead to political unification? Had the accomplishments in life-style, art, literature, education, commerce, law, diplomacy, political astuteness, secular outlook, administrative skill, even in military aptitudes exhausted the country's spiritual potential?[8] Whatever the answer, neither any elementary sense of competition with neighboring peoples, nor humiliating defeats, nor the articulate voices of their political thinkers,[9] and certainly not the ever-present Past were able to overcome Italy's regional tendencies. Was some ingredient lacking in the Italian makeup that was present in Portugal, Spain, France, and England? Italy's many-centered constellation, far from preserving or reacquiring Roman virtues, had developed graces and achievements unknown to her celebrated forebears. But if national unity escaped the Italians, national consciousness was as present here as in other countries, and was as persistent as it was pervasive. Their writers used the word *Italy* quite naturally, their political theorists concerned themselves regularly with problems and dangers facing the whole country:[10] particularism can flourish side by side with comprehension of a greater unit.[11] Nor did foreign admirers and foreign haters of all things Italian distinguish among cities either.[12] The references, for better and for worse, were to Italy, to the Italians.

So long as Italy suffered as the battlefield of competing invaders, she had been granted the independence to decide with whom to ally herself and against whom to fight. But when France and Spain signed the Treaty of Cateau-Cambrésis in 1559, when France withdrew and left Spain in sole command of the peninsula, it meant that Italy had peace, but at the expense of her political existence. This made little difference to the expressions of all-Italian thought. Now, as before 1559, concerns fluctuated among vague hope, shame, nostalgia for the glorious past, and dark despair, not to speak of scorn and hatred for the foreigners. We find it all in Machiavelli, who had died long before 1559, in 1527. In one of his dialogues he puts these words in a participant's mouth: "I don't wish to dismay you... by Italy's condition.... This land seems to be born to raise up dead things, as she did in poetry, painting, and sculpture.... But I am advanced in years and have little hope."[13] His burning desire that the downward course of the country would be reversed was expressed when he was in and out of office, in books, memoranda, and correspondence. Darker feelings, shame and disgust, found utterance in letters such as the one to Vettori: "As to Italy's unity, you make me laugh.... There never will be union here for anything good."[14] Or, a few days later: "I am now ready to weep with you over our ruin and servitude, which, even if it does not come today or tomorrow, will still come in our time."[15] Machiavelli's outburst of hatred for Italy's oppressors is well known. In the last chapter of *The Prince,* he tries to arouse the readers' patriotic emotions, saying that the barbarian domination "stinks in everybody's nose," and he ends the work with an equally patriotic quatrain by Petrarch.[16] And there is the letter to Guicciardini where he exhorts: "Free Italy from her long pains, root out the monster that, except for face and voice, has nothing human in it."[17]

Guicciardini, given his many official duties outside of Tuscany, would no doubt have outgrown parochial thinking soon enough, even if his intelligence had not accomplished this for him in the first place. He could therefore write a history of Italy when "only municipal history had been known in Italy until then."[18] In him, too, slender hope alternated with profound sadness as he faced the political reality of Italy and the insignificant results of his incessant efforts on her behalf. Thus, he wrote down for himself:[19] "Three things I would like to see before I die, but I doubt that I shall see any of them, even if I lived a long time: in our city, the life of a well-ordered republic; Italy freed from all barbarians; and the world delivered from the tyranny of wicked priests."[20]

How tattered the country's fabric, how frayed the sensibilities of its most thoughtful citizens, is shown by the fact that Machiavelli and Guicciardini were frequently busy on diplomatic missions soliciting foreign powers to intervene in support of one ailing side of Italy against another.[21] However, these two men's understanding of Italy's predicament and their endeavors to remedy it are common knowledge. There were other Italians, forgotten today, or known for other reasons, whose words must find a place here. Laments and protestations against selfish princes and foreign exploiters assume a special importance in an atmosphere where fateful decisions and constantly shifting alliances confused the citizens' sense of allegiance. The voices of resistance must be heard against the quiet of the imposed peace and the ready servility of princes and intellectuals.[22]

Four studies by three Italian authors have brought together an impressive number of forgotten names of the period, all of whom were deeply concerned with Italy's fate.[23] These four investigations were published between 1924 and 1936, at a time of renewed "Roman" pride and imperial delusions in Italy. Therefore, the trustworthiness of such studies would tend to be suspect; their purposes might have been opportunistic. Although it was not possible to locate all the sources mentioned in these articles, those I was able to read showed that the original intentions of the sixteenth-century authors had not once been subverted by twentieth-century political motives. The three Italian scholars have not avoided the unpleasant task of naming those who fell over each other to eulogize foreign victors, or those who joined in the prevailing mood of despondency.

Relying on the four works as much as possible, I have put together the following list. It will be seen that five themes are constantly reiterated by the patriots: complaints about the country's disunity; denunciations of popes or princes for having called in the foreigners; regrets about unhappy Italy, once so great, now so humiliated; curses against the transalpines, the barbarians;[24] appeals for unity. There are also two proposals for liberation and confederation of Italy.

LUDOVICO ARIOSTO (1474-1533), in the *Orlando Furioso,* prophesies that one day Italy will be freed from the French (13. 60); reflects on the tyrants who made "our Italy" a bleeding prey (17. 2); deplores that drunken Italy sleeps instead of grieving that she had become a servant to those who once were under her command (17. 75 ff); predicts that the French lily will, as in the past and in vain, seek to plant its withered roots in Italian soil (33. 8 ff); and mourns for Italy, starved, soiled by harpies. Her cruel fate will come to an end once she shakes off her leaden slumber and stirs her sons to action with reminders of the heroic deeds of their ancestors (34. 1-3). All the deeds that Ariosto praises and recommends are extracted from classical mythology, not from the history of Italy. (Cian 1924, pp. 145 ff.)

PIERNO BELLI (1502-1575) was a jurist who wrote on international law before Grotius. In his *De re' militari et bello tractatus* (1563), he finds space to deplore the conditions and the desolation of poor Italy whom too many masters enslaved after she had been mistress of the human race. (Belli 1936, p. 147; English translation, p. 335).

MATTEO-MARIA BOIARDO (1441?-1494) interrupted the *Orlando Innamorato* presumably on account of the French invasion, as he explains in the next to the last stanza: "While I sing . . . I see that the French get all excited to ruin the beautiful land Italy. . . ."[25]

BALDASSARE CASTIGLIONE (1478-1525). In book 1, chapter 34 of the *Cortigiano,* one speaker thinks that too much learning has undermined Italy's willingness to fight. But "the cause of our ruin and our debased, if not dead, virtues" must be attributed to certain leaders. In book 2, chapter 26, another speaker blames Italian affection for Spanish and French fashions: better to look less fasionable, wear your own style, and so signal your liberty. Imitation is a sign of servility. Later on, in book 4, chapter 4, the courtly behavior that disgraced the Italian name is discussed: Italians have become effeminate through the affectation of so much polish and no longer risk their lives. Finally, in the same fourth book, chapter 33, great wealth is said to have caused Italy's downfall: "Poor Italy that was and still is the prey of foreigners, as much through bad government as through too much wealth." (Cian 1924, p. 186.)

PIETRO CRINITO (1475-1507), whose real name was Ricci, wrote Latin poetry. In one work, "Ad Faustum, de Carlo rege francorum cum ad urbem tenderet cum exercitu," he vented his hatred of the French hordes that swarmed down upon and threatened Naples, while sluggish Italy became the laughingstock of the world. (Cian 1924, p. 155. Estienne Pasquier singles out both Crinito and Giovio[see below] for particularly unpleasant anti-French arrogance, in *Recherches* 1. 2.)

TEOFILO FOLENGO (1496-1544) has one of the Furies of his *Il Baldus* (25. 346-50), brag about her success in sowing the seeds of discord in Italy. Then, changing his tone, the poet exclaims, "Italians who once were strong enough to conquer the world are divided today and have become serfs, vassals, and servants to those who had been their vassals, serfs and servants." (Cian 1924, pp. 152-53.)

GERONIMO FRACASTORO (1478-1553), the doctor-poet, breaks into a passionate lament in the midst of his scientific epic, *Sifilis sive de morbo gallico* (1. 420-69). He lovingly remembers the peaceful country, so rich in land, climate, art, and heroes. But now: "Who can find words to describe our shame? The Gallic King has come and oppressed region after region, so that the whole country now lies in tears and pains." (Cian 1924, p. 152.)

PAOLO GIOVIO (1483-1552) the historian, praised Italian and foreign captains equitably, in his *Vite del Gran Capitano e del Marchese Pescara*. Yet he too was sensitive to his country's misery. He wished, he says in book 1, chapter 2, and again in chapter 9, that Fate had endowed afflicted Italy a captain like the Gran Capitano (the Spaniard, Gonzalvo Córdoba). With the help of such a hero, the loss of liberty due to our mad dissensions that have also cost us the ancient military repute and all respect in the world could be remedied.

LODOVICO DOMENICHI (1515-1564) rendered Giovio's Latin biographies into Italian. He translated many works but also wrote poetry. In one of his sonnets he implores God to avenge Italy's servitude, to take away the yoke that the sons of the Rhine and the Ebro had placed on her neck destroying her pleasant fields. (Cf. Cian 1924, p. 157, who might, however, refer to another, still angrier poem.)

DONATO GIANNOTTI (1494-1563)—like Machiavelli before him, a Florentine and Secretary of the Ten, and like Machiavelli, exiled—dedicated to Pope Paul III a *Discorso delle cose d'Italia*. Here he developed a proposal for uniting Italian princes through warfare against the emperor, who at this juncture, 1553, seemed to Giannotti the more dangerous of the country's various occupiers. He counseled the pope to call upon England or France for help in chasing out the emperor. The Italian princes were to prepare themselves for an offensive war, which, if it seemed harsh at first, promised to be rewarded by sweet victory and finally freedom. He added, however, that he doubted that the princes would understand the timely wisdom of such a proposal.(Cf. Curcio 1934, p. 182; and Starn 1968, pp. 43 ff.)

ORAZIO LANDO (1512?-1555?), the polygrapher, was perhaps not too deeply stirred by Italy's misfortune. He might merely have been following the fashion when he praised ancient Rome as "nurse of the world, elected by God to unite the separate dominions, to soften crude customs of barbarians, to become the common fatherland of the human race." This eulogy of a great history is contained in his *Commentario delle più notabili e monstruose cose d'Italia...*, of 1548, where he contrasted the shining past with the "monstruous" state of the present. (Curcio 1934, p. 184; and, for Lando's life and character: Grendler 1969, pp. 71 ff.)

GIROLOAMO MUZIO JUSTINOPOLITANO (1496-1576), man of letters and courtier, submitted a proposal for Italy's salvation to another pope, Pius IV. The short treatise—it is contained in some seven pages—is simple and commonsensical. Muzio thought that the pope, as the only power of any stability in Italy, should initiate the planned confederation. Local princes, and he counted among them the ruling Spanish king, would keep their present possessions but would contribute men and money to a common pool. Practical details will have to be worked out by experts, but, he says, if the rude Swiss with their many cantons have achieved unity, even under the strain of religious dissension, the more refined Italians should certainly be able to do the same. The time is ripe for rallying all those of good will, all those who are concerned in the face of the open-mouthed wolf eager to swallow the country. He closes the proposal by imploring the pope to fulfill his office as head of Italy as well as of the Church, respected as he is in this quality by all nations, assured as he can be that his name will be immortalized on earth "as father and conserver of the Italian state." This *Discorso del Mutio Iustinopolitano...per la unione d'Italia,* part of a work called *Selva Odorifera,* was published in 1572, long after the Pope's death. In his later correspondence with the Grand Duke of Florence, Muzio is much more outspoken in his national views. He keeps reminding Duke Francesco de' Medici of the urgent need for Italian unity, for getting rid of all foreigners. In one of these letters (November, 1574), he exclaims: "How beautiful, how happy would Italy be if she were returned to her own government and could be enjoyed by Italians as France is being enjoyed by the French, Spain by the Spaniards, Germany by the Germans. . . . Great is our misery because this country, once queen of all kingdoms, must today play the role of servant to foreign and barbaric nations. Our sins have blinded us, our blindness keeps us subjected." (Tocco 1924 and 1926, p. 34; Curcio 1934, pp. 188 ff.)

PAOLO PARUTA (1540?-1598), the Venetian historian, may not have had all-Italian considerations in mind. His constant comparisons between the greatness of Venice and that of ancient Rome seemed compulsive and always to the advantage of the former. He certainly intended to elevate the rank of Venice as well, when he stressed the city's role in the interest of Italian freedom and glory, but it is noteworthy that such claims for national endeavors were apparently expected of an historian. In many of his *Discorsi politici,* he disputed the oft-repeated assertion that Venetian actions were selfish, claiming that they benefited Italy as a whole. "How much care has she not taken for the liberty and glory of Italy, when she went to war to protect Naples and Milan," he wrote in the first discourse of book 2. And again, in the following discourse, he praised Venice for having supported Pisa "for the liberty of all Italy." In the ninth discourse of book 2, Paruta rethought Leo X's decision to ally himself with one foreign power in order to banish the other, and he praises the pope's decision because "to throw out the transalpines was the desire of all Italians."

MARIN SANUDO (1466-1535), another Venetian, mixed local history with all-Italian concern as easily as Paruta in a diary that he dedicated, in 1495, to the Doge, under the title *La Spedizione di Carlo VIII.* He had begun the diary the previous year, the year of the French invasion of Venice. And Sanudo wrote that it was clear from the beginning that this was not a localized calamity but one that endangered all Italy. He could only trust in God to take care of this most beautiful part of the inhabited world, for He had placed the Alps in the north for no other purpose than to separate Italians from the barbarians.[26] The French would soon enough be stripped of their Italian conquests just as they had been before.

DOMENICO VENIERO (1517-1582), a Venetian poet, wrote a sonnet (*Rime*, p. 25) about the desperate straits of "unhappy Italy, divided against herself, that cannot win without losing, not be hurt in one part without hurting the whole body. Neither Emperor nor French King had come to Italy for the country's benefit. How could she have abandoned her defenses into such hands!"

The four studies here so abundantly exploited also contain, besides other authors, anonymous pieces and popular songs, all full of patriotic feelings.[27]

The controversy between the proponents of Latin and those of the vernacular had, like so much else, begun in Italy.[28] Mother tongues everywhere defied the cultural prerogatives of the ancient language, the erudite craze for the recently acquired more genuine Latin, and the undeniable practicality of a lingua franca. Those who did write in the vernacular often felt bound to justify their decision. Sanudo, for example, said that he preferred to be read by many instead of exhausting himself in the service of a handful of readers (*La Spedizione*, 19). Vettori mentioned negligently that, of course, Latin would have been the more distinguished mode of writing, but it would not have brought him many readers. He said he enjoyed writing in Italian more (*Sommario*, dedicatory letter). Others said so too, but a particularly extensive and subtle explanation for using his native language appears in Paruta's prefatory letter to his *Degli Istorici*, 19-25, which demonstrates the difficulties of saying in Latin what had been thought out and felt in Italian.[29] It also seemed to Paruta more appropriate to write about an Italian city (Venice) in Italian, for "Italy's true glory" (*Degli Istorici*, 14). Ariosto, on the other hand, said in the introduction to his comedy *Cassaria* that, for a comedy, Italian was surely good enough. But "surely," the author of *Orlando Furioso* could not have taken his own words too seriously.

In Italy, the general European problem acquired special features. Here the philologists quarreled endlessly about the respective standing of several dialects.[30] And only here were both Latin and Italian indigenous languages. The preservation of Latin had become a truly pathetic quest for the salvation of a last shred of patrimony from general debacle. What Valla had written 100 years earlier (above, p. 29), can be heard again in Sigognio (1513-1584), the medievalist-archivist, who, in 1556, implored a group of young Venetian noblemen to hold fast to the ancient language to prevent what "has already happened to the Imperium, so that also the glory of our Roman language might become transferred to foreign lands. No other vestige is left us of the pristine liberty, of the old graces, of Italy's ancient dignity. Nothing but this most honored patrimony with which [Rome] once gave the law to the surface of the earth."[31] Similarly, Giovio deplored the theft of so many valuables from Italian soil. The little that remained, Italy's ancient "eloquence," should be safeguarded religiously: "We still hold the citadel of the pure and reliable speech with which... traditional Roman decency, unconquerably preserved, holds out against the foreigners. It now behooves every good citizen, for eternal pride, to watch fullheartedly over what is left from the riches of our ancestors."[32] And again, another Italian, Doni, mourned the death of the printer Aldo Manuzio, who, while alive, did not allow Latin to escape from "its own nest" to look for a new home abroad.[33]

No protest in verse or prose, in Italian or Latin, led to any course of action. "The dream of 'Italian liberty' survived, but only as an ever emptier literary reminiscense.... 'Italian liberty' was nothing but a rhetorical and false euphemism: it lost ever more its old meaning of chasing out the foreigner, and became synonymous for 'Italian quietude,' according to the directions of Emperor Charles V and obeyed by his Italian officials."[34] Tocco, many years earlier, had come to the same conclusion, except that he had stressed the country's permanent consciousness of a particular character, a consciousness which kept the unifying idea of freedom breathing throughout the years of foreign rule.[35]

When Italy had to endure new hardships in the twentieth century—Fascism, war, and defeat—another Italian, Alexandre d'Entrèves, reflected once more on his country's condition. Tying together ancient Rome, Dante, Machiavelli, and the *Risorgimento,* he marveled at Italy's survival, attributing it to the continuity of a national consciousness: "The idea of a nation as a spiritual unit ... might well be the Italian answer to the foreign idols of a community of blood and soil."[36]

The country's difficulty in creating a nation-state led observers from more successful nations to scorn even these sterile Italian attempts over the centuries. Failure is so easily seen as a deficiency also of intention. That equation is certainly unjustified, but, then, failure, like success, has its own consequences.

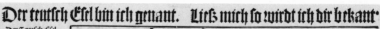

"*The German Ass, I am called....,*" broadsheet c. 1560.

Germany

Despite a past so unlike Italy's, Germany had evolved into a similar country politically: divided and reluctant to accept unified rule. In a paradoxical sense, Italy was in better straits, for she was distracted by foreign domination from more suicidal politics, while the Germans, uninvaded, masters at home, became increasingly alienated from one another with the advent of the Reformation. The roots of the German failure to maintain their medieval hegemony in Europe, to develop as had their western neighbors, have been seen in the prolonged absences of their medieval emperors, in their involvements in Italy and in their unsuccessful clashes with the popes. Dependent on peace at home and needing support for their undertakings, the distant emperors were forced to pay for help with cessations of lands, titles, and privileges.[1] The free election of emperors has also been regarded as a disruptive element compared with the more stable system of hereditary monarchy.[2] These are, indeed, important factors in Germany's history of disunity. But a trait we tend to appreciate today, namely a fierce determination to resist domination, was present among the German states, at times assuming the form of honest political concern, at times becoming a pretext for lawless actions.[3] The attempt to impress their rulers with their right to participate in government had a long history among the territorial princes. It might well be called the salient feature of German politics during the sixteenth century. It did not work out well for the country as a whole, its entire history being too crowded with complexities and perplexities.[4] It was Germany's fate to combine longsightedness (for instance, lingering imperial, "Roman," aspirations)[5] with nearsightedness (the particularism that finally led to political checkmate).[6]

If necessity created talents, as is often assumed, the country lying in the center of Europe would, above all others, have developed a special gift for power politics. But difficulties began with the fixing of exact boundaries to the Empire.[7] Another complication, a collision rather, stemmed from the question of which territories belonged to the Empire, the *Reich*, and which were family property of the Habsburgs, their *Hausmacht*. Only the combination of emperorship and *Hausmacht* had sufficient weight in Europe, and so they were, for practical purposes, indispensable to each other.[8] Indeed, sizable possessions—land and subjects—gave an imperial candidate a favorable position in the calculations of electors and estates.[9] But then this very accumulation of power aroused fear inside the *Reich* as among its neighbors. Only a German was to hold the exalted office of emperor,[10] and the elected swore, among other things, to extend and not to alienate the imperial lands, as well as to regain lost ones.[11] The imperial letterheads quite regularly bore the partial title "Increaser of the Empire."

Thus it would appear that the emperor was not to be a mere figurehead, but the country's master and protector of its patrimony. Yet, no sooner was a ruler crowned than he was stripped of all effectiveness by the estates' rejection of most of the proposals and requirements presented to them at the Imperial Diets. The contradictory impulses in Germany can best be observed in the wearisome election of Charles V and in its aftermath.[12] From beginning to end of his long reign, the emperor would meet with opposition from vested interests unwilling to surrender any privileges to imperial prerogatives, as well as from Protestant resistance to his determination to crush this heresy.[13]

Also paradoxical is the fact that Germany, while shying away from hereditary kingship, uninterruptedly from 1438 on, chose her emperors among the Habsburg family. And not one of the five Habsburgs who ruled during the sixteenth century was born in Germany proper.[14] It seems no less strange that there were cities in the land designated for imperial elections, for coronations, for the seat of the Supreme Judicial Chamber, for the Diets, but none for any central administrations, or for a fixed residence of emperors.[15]

The task set for the successors of the Roman Empire and of Charlemagne was more than a paradox; it was something of an attempt of squaring the circle. Maximilian I and Charles V—and we can restrict ourselves to these two emperors, the last to play an important role in the Europe of the period—were regarded by themselves and others as divinely destined reuniters of the faith and of the dispersed lands owing allegiance to the imperial crown; as liberators, conditions permitting, of Christian areas fallen to the Turks;[16] and also, understandably, as caretakers of the family possessions.[17] If Maximilian's reign was scintillating and adventurous, yet of uncertain significance for Germany,[18] Charles' charges were altogether unmanageable.

As king of Spain he had to satisfy Spanish interests,[19] which were not congruent with his obligations to Germany.[20] Even had he not had worldwide duties, Charles did not feel close to the country that, more than anything, needed a full-time ruler.[21] He knew little German when he became Emperor and hardly had time to acquaint himself with the land during his always stormy duty stops there. He succeeded in shaping himself into a truly Spanish king; he tamed the Italian disorders, and he worsted the French again and again. But he could not deal with this strange, strong, populous Germany, with its efficiently run cities, and—least of all—with its headstrong princes.[22] The princes had been left to their own devices for so long that a king with any hope of molding them into a workable unit would have had to remain on the spot, concentrating on German affairs.[23] And how much more essential was his presence when a religious volcano was about to erupt. Yet, to the historians' surprise, the Empire held together for 300 years more,[24] despite its endemic ills, the religious schism, and its numerous independent elements: towns, estates, princes, knights, electors, and, in the background, the population at large. The binding forces included a number of traditional institutions,[25] fear of the Turks in the East and of the French in the West, political and economical opposition to papal Rome, and, as far as it went, resentment toward the cultural arrogance of Italian humanists. Such resentment on the part of erudite Germans was certainly unimportant quantitatively, but the learned circles represented Germany's most articulate voices, and their "secret inferiority complex with regard to the Italians,"[26] fueled the passionate study and praise of their land and their past.

Basically, therefore, the Empire was able to maintain its identity throughout a stormy period because of a sense of nationalism, which was no stronger and no weaker than that of other countries. Political disjointedness is evidently no obstacle to racial or national pride. If the present is too worrisome, the past is available for proof of superiority. Ironically, Germany had what the Italian patriots so fervently longed for: a single sovereign, an emperor. So we find another paradox. However brittle the significance of the title in practical respects, it had preserved its aura and was a unifying agent.[27] "The Emperor is the Empire," a fourteenth-century writer had declared.[28] It did not matter that even then the equation was not true.

When, in 1493, Maximilian I arrived on the scene, replacing his father and ending a long, lethargic reign, Germany was electrified by the change of pace, the sudden visibility of the emperor and his colorful personality. Maximilian intended to impress the world and to make his weight felt at home in the exhausting struggle with the princes who both needed and opposed him. With talent and energy, he used printing press and writers to propagate his ideas, thus to reach the common people and circumvent the Diets to which he would have to submit requests, to establish a genealogy worthy of his ancient house, and, finally, to prepare works of art and books designed to make his name immortal.[29]

The German humanists supported him enthusiastically, and he, in turn, flattered them with his attention, consulting and employing the learned, and crowning poets. The happy relationship was not unlike that of Francis I, a few years later, and his French humanists.

German humanists, like those elsewhere, had learned their humanities in Italy; and it was one Italian in particular, Aeneas Silvius Piccolomini, who had vouched for the moral and martial accomplishments of their German forebears and for the cultural progress of Germany in the time since Tacitus had described that land in all its roughness (in the *Germania*).[30] It had been Piccolomini's intention to flatter the Germans of the previous century into supporting a papal crusade against the Turks; he succeeded in launching German humanists, after some delay, into an extensive investigation of whatever could be found about their country, past and present. The romantic infatuation with their ancestors was in degree and kind equal to the patriotic effusions of the nineteenth century.[31] In addition, there was nothing particularly German about this ardor; we find the same self-glorification in all other European countries of the time.

In Germany it was not necessary, as it was in Italy, to leap back across a thousand-year span to resurrect a monarchical tradition. Whatever the splintered state of their political affairs, German humanists could refer with supreme ease to their Empire. Even when concerned with a regional question, they did not lose sight of the greater aggregate. When, for example, Jacob Wimpfeling (1450-1528) argued for the rights of his native Alsatia and against French pretensions to ownership of the left bank of the Rhine, he demonstrated that Alsatia had at all times belonged to the German emperors, that it was part of the *Reich*.[32] When Conrad Celtis (1459-1508) wrote a history of Nuremberg,[33] he intended it to be part of a description of the whole of Germany, a *Germania illustrata*.[34] He bequeathed the project to his friends and disciples, and if they did not bring it off, it was most certainly not for want of love for the subject. We find this patriotic trend again in

Heinrich Bebel (1472-1516), a Swabian who wrote a eulogy of Swabia and the Swabians.[35] The rest of his lifework, in verse and in prose, was devoted to paying unstinting homage to the German nation and its culture.[36]

One more humanist-imperialist, Ulrich von Hutten (1488-1523), deserves singling out from the band of like-minded Germans.[37] While in the service of Archibshop Albrecht of Mainz, he composed a 1300-line panegyric for his master that almost immediately widened into an epic of German history.[38] Hutten's short, staccato life ended in misery and exile, but in the time allowed him, this musketeer among the humanists blasted away at the enemies of the Holy German Empire: the Turks, the Pope, the exploitative churchmen, and the selfish, squabbling, gluttonous German princes, who had forgotten what they owed emperor, people, and forebears, as well as their ancient military valor. In an oration prepared for the Augsburg Diet of 1518, Hutten expressed all of his and his fellow-patriots' grievances.[39] Here he also seized upon a current rumor of possible foreign succession to the imperial throne,[40] reminding the electors of the shame of having an alien emperor (p. 131), especially for the Germans, a people indigenous to the soil they inhabited—they had Tacitus' word for it—and from which they had expanded and conquered in all directions, yet remained immune to foreignness. The main thrust of Hutten's argument lay in the exhortation to the assembled princes to take up arms against the Turks, to lead the German youth into battle, to seize the unique opportunity of diverting the idle and the poor from thoughts of revolt and guiding them into noble and invigorating action (pp. 101, 133). Unite, unite, he adjures the princes: *we are all branches of one tree* (p. 117; my emphasis). Follow your superb monarch under whose guidance you will defeat the Turks and save Germany as well as Christianity. There was nothing in the exhortation that other German humanists would not and did not propound.

For the politically and historically inclined humanist, who had spent long years in his Latin universe, the historic moment of truth had for a long time been the "Transfer of

Empire" in the fifth century, or, more officially, Charlemagne's coronation at Rome in the ninth.[41] The identification of the Holy German Empire with the Roman Empire had, by sheer repetition, become reflexive, self-evident. Today's Germans were the new Romans, who, never defeated, had assumed the abundant mantle of glory and the custodial responsibility for the rest of the world (e.g., Hutten's oration; p. 125). They all saw that the country was in bad shape, but other than wringing their hands, their only response to this insight was reminding their countrymen of the imperial past and of their racial superiority.[42] World dominance, they held, was theirs by right. The dream of continuing Roman universality and the fact of Charlemagne's protection of the Church informed the rhetoric of the emperors, probably through conviction, and assuredly through education.[43] But the harsh realities of German politics, and of the rulers' own precarious position, had taught them to use another appeal, the appeal to national sensitivity.

Whether imperial expressions of love and devotion for country and people were more heartfelt than protestations of concern for Church and Christian man's soul cannot be determined. It is likely that Maximilian had enough contact with all levels of the population, having traveled widely in Germany, to acquire some feeling for the nation.[44] It is unlikely that Charles understood what the term "national feeling" meant, he whose grand servants had names like Alba, Croy, Chièvres, Gattinara, Granvelle, de los Cobos; he who was obsessed with Spain and her colonial empire, with Italy, and with his bitter wars with France. In Germany, the hostile princes and the Protestants set themselves against him. Twice it came to war. Twice the princes sought support from his archenemy, the French king. If we encounter in the emperors' official pronouncements frequent expressions directed at the "nation," we can assume that they were timely and regarded as useful.

Maximilian stressed in many mandates that Germany's honor was his own, that he would see to it that Germany's enemies should no longer dare despise the German nation or wash their hands in German blood.[45] He had Germany's well-being on his mind. He, as well as his hereditary lands, were Germany's bulwarks against aggressors.[46] From the beginning of his reign, he had worked to protect the Christian Empire, to preserve and augment its honor, its well-being.[47] He urged princes and estates to support his unwavering defense of all things German.[48] He reminded them of the many Diets he had summoned for the sole purpose of asking for understanding and help in his efforts to hold and strengthen the frontiers, to keep the crown in German hands. He was working tirelessly for the country and had managed to protect the Empire so far. He urged the estates or individual princes to remember the threats from the Turks and from the French, of the danger of losing the crown and the Empire altogether.[49] The French were preparing to steal the crown from the Germans,[50] and Maximilian was ready to perform any sacrifice for the Holy Empire and for the German nation, and so, he vowed, would his successors.[51] Admonishing the Swiss not to soldier for the French king, he also warned them that the French were scheming to usurp the imperial crown from the Germans. The honor and success of the Empire and the German nation were his own.[52] So we read in one missive after another.

Here is how Charles, as yet only king of Spain, solicited electors for his candidacy to the emperorship. He believed himself the worthiest of the contenders because "not only were We born of German blood and ancestry but because our ancestors, the Roman emperors, ruled the Empire most skillfully.... So, We too, once We will be honored by the office, will take best care of the peace and well-being of the German nation ... for the eternal glory of the Holy Roman Empire and of the German nation."[53] Years later, in dealing with the rebellious princes, he wrote to the estates to convince them of his paternal fidelity to and affection for the German nation, their common fatherland. He protested his unceasing efforts in their behalf: he wanted to preserve their liberties.[54] Again, a few years later, and once more in a military confrontation with the princes, he sent a message to one of them in which he emphasized his long patience with the French king, who was always the aggressor, constantly attempting to toss the German nation—the eternal defender of Christianity—to the Turks. The French king depicted their emperor, who was elected by the German nation and is himself of German blood, as the enemy of the common welfare, as the oppressor of the traditional German liberties, whereas he, Charles, always had uppermost in his mind the German nation's honor and well-being, as well as the protection of its traditional freedom.[55] In a reply to complaints by the estates, the emperor assured them that, far from intending to diminish their freedoms or those of the German nation, his "beloved fatherland," he desired to protect and preserve them.[56]

In 1552, the emperor had lost the battle in Germany. In accepting the peace agreements, he said that he had never wished to bring war to the Holy German nation, "Our beloved Fatherland."[57] His brother Ferdinand, who had worked out the peace treaty with the German princes, declared in the emperor's name that peace and concord in the "German Empire, his beloved fatherland," had always been his [the Emperor's] ambition.[58]

The printing presses were busy spreading far and wide the polemics of the time. Pamphlets supporting and opposing the imperial party became repositories of limitless patriotic posturings. Propaganda campaigns accompanied battles and accords and gathered around the heroes and villains of the moment. The publicists for the emperor underlined his close ties with the German nation, his endeavor to bring religious peace to the country and to preserve the traditional freedoms. He and his house were ready to sacrifice everything for the fatherland.[59] "O noble fatherland," another leaflet read, "open your eyes to see with what slyness the French and their allies [the German princes] attempt to anguish your bodies and souls. The French persecute the Protestants at home. But you, German princes, are too weak unless you find outside help. You protest the sight of Spaniards, the 'black heads,' in Germany. Had you obeyed your emperor, he would not have needed his faithful Spaniards...." And so it went on, the imperial propagandists stressing the emperor's love for Germany, in general, and for German liberties, in particular, as well as his efforts to keep the country free from Turks and Frenchmen.[60]

The imperialists also strongly stressed that the emperor did not fight the princes because of religious persuasion, but because they were rebels against their sovereign, treacherously allying themselves with his and Germany's enemies. This last point should not be overlooked, for alliances with foreign powers against one's sovereign were regarded as treason: they were certainly not considered normal in the sixteenth century.[61] The reaction of the betrayed emperor was repeated in popular songs and in contemporary opinion, as was reported, for instance, by a Protestant English observer, Roger Ascham, who tried hard to clear one of the leading Protestant warlords of treason.[62] As a warning to German soldiers who might contemplate going into French service, Charles ordered the trial and subsequent execution of a captain of the mercenaries who had been on the French payroll.[63] The warlords' delivery to France of a number of German towns that were not theirs to give stimulated immediate popular condemnation.[64] So princes were considered traitors on the basis of their friendship with France, but condemnation of the emperor for having Italians and Spaniards as advisers or soldiers, or for his alliance with the Antichrist, the Pope, was no less severe.[65]

Popular songs and pamphlets stressed the religious question, while the anti-imperial propaganda of the princes concerned itself with the need for liberation from the "beastly servitude" imposed by a tyrant. Here follow a few examples of the songs.[66] "O God Father of Jesus Christ / Who are father of the wise / I pray to you from the bottom of my heart ... / My fatherland is oppressed ... / I will wear no finery on my body [a young girl is speaking] / Until Germany is free again ... / May my dear fatherland / Be rescued from the Spaniards' hands."[67] The devil, the emperor, and their cohorts have "betrayed this fatherland."[68] "They have ravaged and destroyed the dear German land.../ They are the evil Christians/ That have destroyed Germany."[69]

The mercenaries' songs combined faith and martial determination: "The noble German land is mine/ Is our fatherland alone... let all who turn to you [to Christ]/ Increase in fear and love of you./ Take away our sorrow and shame/ Grant that we may honor our fatherland through Christ."[70] Or this warning to the world: "No leader ever in the world/ Has opposed the Germans/ But was in due time defeated."[71] And: "Cheer up, you German Christians/ For the time has come.../ Take up your arms.../ Help save God's honor/ ... and the fatherland's.../ The emperor wants to use force against us good free Germans/ And take away our ancient liberties/ Under false semblance/ Godless traitors of the *Reich* are they."[72]

Then there were Moritz, the Saxonian Elector and cool political adventurer, and Albrecht Alcibiades, the erratic condottiere and Markgrave of Brandenburg-Kulmbach.[73] Both Protestants, they fought, like many Protestants, on the emperor's side in the Schmalcaldic War that resulted in 1547 in an imperial victory. The two men then switched loyalties and played their parts in the anti-Charles, anti-Habsburg conspiracy of 1552-1553. Moritz's name figures prominently in the Chambord Treaty with Henry II of France,[74] and, on several occasions, Albrecht had been sent off to France for preliminary talks about the alliance. Albrecht, however, occupied himself chiefly with pillaging and blackmailing German cities. Following Charles' defeat by the coalition and withdrawal from Germany, and after his brother Ferdinand had been elected emperor in his stead, Moritz joined the imperial party again to fight the Turks, dropping his French interests. He was finally forced to turn upon and die fighting the brazen Albrecht, who in turn had to flee Germany. He too died shortly thereafter. At their deaths, the two men were still in their thirties, and Charles in Yuste must have had his moment of satisfaction.

No biographer has detected a trace of religious or national conviction in either man; we would be hard put to extract much of any emotion other than ambition in Moritz's correspondence (which was of a strictly political nature).[75] Therefore, the elevated concern with religion and fatherland evinced in his public statements, intended to justify his taking up arms against Charles after having fought for him, stands out startlingly. In such delicate matters as changing sides and allying oneself with the enemy, the tone is likely to be sonorous. And so we find Moritz, along with the cosignatories of the Chambord Treaty with the French king, accusing the emperor not only of suppressing the new faith but also of subjecting the people of "our dear fatherland Germany" to "beastly servitude." The terms "beloved fatherland" and "German liberty" appear more than once in the document. The same moral indignation animates a manifest that Moritz sent to the estates, explaining his motives and inviting them to join the coalition. Along with another attack on the emperor for persecuting the faithful, he charged him with other misdeeds of utter gravity for Germany, "mother of us all," such as allowing foreign troops to be stationed on German soil and permitting them to ravage the countryside. Interspersed in the text are charges that Germany was financially exploited and numerous expressions of Moritz's concern for German liberties. If the estates would join the coalition, he suggested, they would be welcome; if not, no house of theirs would be immune to punishment.[76] In the same year, 1552, Moritz made a speech in which he rises to still greater heights of patriotism and xenophobia.[77]

As for Albrecht's pronouncements, they are equally chauvinistic, and they are perhaps the most impudent of all paradings of national feeling, considering his exploits in the service of the country's enemies and participation in the pillaging of German lands. He too felt it incumbent upon him to explain why he turned against the emperor and sought French assistance. In a manifest of 1552,[78] he enumerated Charles' offenses against Germany's rights and freedoms: the religious have been persecuted; foreigners have the upper hand in Germany, despite the emperor's formal promises;[79] the presence of foreign troops on German soil, where they have done untold damage to the fields, is unlawful even in peacetime; one has to learn foreign languages to be heard at court; the long-standing right of Germans to take service in other nations' armies has been denied them; territorial princes have been forbidden to put their portraits on coins. Yes, servitude has been inflicted on Germany. A history of the Schmalcaldic campaign written by one of the emperor's generals has been published, and with the emperor's approval [here certain German soldiers, Albrecht among them, all of whom fought on the Emperor's side, had been portrayed in a less than flattering light]. Within its pages, Albrecht exclaimed, "Germany the most noble and distinguished nation in Christendom," is described as if she were an unknown, barbaric country. After an outburst against greedy prelates, Albrecht invited the estates and princes to join the alliance. Otherwise, they could expect persecution with fire and blood.[80] During one of his punitive actions against Nuremberg, he summoned the city to fulfill his demands "in the name of the King of France and our alliance," for "German liberty," and in the interest of religion.[81]

Hypocrisy is, we know, an homage that vice pays to virtue. The cynicism of the last texts at least shows us what constituted the proper tone and proper arguments in the propaganda war between emperor and warlords. But such cynicism is not all that is available to us; we can also hear an earnest, modest, devout, and quite frightened expression of love for the fatherland in the historian Sleidan. Anti-Roman and suspicious of the emperor though he was, he described the Empire as a fragile gift that God had bestowed on the Germans, as undeservedly as He had once granted it to Rome, a gift to be used warily, since it was the last of the four great world monarchies.[82]

Attitudes and vocabulary were altered by the turmoils. We hear very little any more of the Holy Roman Empire in the tracts, nothing about Germany's world-embracing role, and absent too is the idolization of the imperial person. If the rhetoric of imperial rights and duties had become moribund, it was due largely to the advent of Luther. Phraseology— whether to warn or to praise—now concerned the country Germany alone, and the emperors' appeals had adapted themselves to this reality. Whatever the new faith meant to the individual Protestant princes and leaders, the now official anti-Roman stance had proved to be a most opportune instrument for anti-Habsburg politics. The religious revolt had unintentionally contributed to making national consciousness more pointedly national.

It would be rash to draw Luther too deeply into the current of bona fide nationalism. He knew, at best, how to utilize the prevailing spirit.[83] Yet nobody did more for the German language, and hardly anyone had more affinity for it. It is a sheer marvel to read in his "Letter on Translation" (*Werke* 30^2, 627-46) of the extraordinary pains he and his helpers took in the continuous revisions of the Bible translation, "searching fourteen days, three to four weeks for a single word, sometimes not finding it.... One must not ask the Latin letter how to speak German.... One must ask the mother in the house, the children in the streets, the ordinary man in the marketplace, look him 'in the mug' [*aufs Maul sehen*] to see how they speak, and translate accordingly. They will then understand and know that one speaks German to them." But for him language, even the German language, was only a tool for a better understanding of the holy texts. He had not appeared on the scene to found German academies. He had confronted the country with problems of another sort.

The propitious hour for German letters had not yet arrived. No German-writing author was laureated as were his Latinist colleagues. Yet much was written in German, of course, and even the humanists exhorted their countrymen to use their own language.[84] They themselves assuredly went on writing in Latin, a matter of convenience if they wanted to be read abroad, and also if they wished to be ranked among the learned. But even here, patriotic motives played their part: German scholars had to prove that they were not barbarians, that they could handle Latin as well as the Italians. Abbot Trithemius (1462-1516), for example, dedicated to his friend Wimpfeling[85] a *Catalogue of Famous German Writers* and deplored the fact that Germany was regarded as a land devoid of art. He had written the *Catalogue,* he said, in opposition to the Rome-worshippers, who suppressed everything favorable relating to Germany.[86] On a later occasion, Trithemius again complained that "Italian and French authors, so zealous when they write about anything that seems to them worthwhile in their own lands, never mention [German accomplishments], spurning, as if by arrangement, everything memorable done by Germans."[87] The geographer-historian, Albert Krantz (d. 1517), accused the Italians of suppressing precious old documents that mention Germany, out of envy.[88] Mutianus Rufus (1471-1526) thought that Germany had nothing to fear in a comparison with Italy. The Germans were no barbarians, but malevolent writers had distorted their attainments.[89] Franz Irenicus (1495-c. 1559) was incensed at the low esteem in which Italians held the German language. He too wanted it known that Germans were not uncivilized.[90] In case Celtis[91] really lectured in German,[92] and if Paracelsus did so too,[93] they might have followed foreign models. But while Italians had begun long ago to form learned societies for the advancement of their mother tongue,[94] Germany had no guiding personality, no forum to support and enhance individual efforts. In Latin and in German, they blamed their countrymen for sluggishness and inability to write as elegantly as others, for the poor impression they made abroad, for ignorance everywhere of German feats and talents.[95] They endeavored with all their might to diminish ancient Rome's importance in the process of civilizing Germany—hitting with the same strokes the presumptuous descendents in Italy. They seized upon favorable remarks in Caesar; they mixed casually Celts, Gauls, and Germans, inventing as their cultural masters the Druids, who, they affirmed, were Greeks chased from their homeland by Tiberius. (The French historians arranged history in the same way, as we will see.) Conrad Celtis was responsible for inventing the Druids for Germany, and he had eager and grateful disciples to spread the finding.[96]

No more proof seems to be needed to show that Germany had its multilayered nationalism too. While the emperor was definitely not the *Reich*,[97] while religion did not belong to the *Reich* either—since it belonged now, after the Augsburg Diet of 1555, to the territorial princes—the sense of national kinship, with all its anguish and all its vainglory, was not in doubt in the sixteenth century.

Portrait of Charles IX of France,

France

Confident opinion holds that countries and peoples have their individual, unmistakable traits, and many theories have been advanced to explain how peoples attained their particular qualities. Climate, geography, and stellar conjunctions have been proposed as reasons, and, at other times, national characteristics have been attributed to economic or social factors. "Unmistakable" traits, however, happen to undergo massive changes through the centuries. In the last 100 years, for example, it had been readily asserted that a "typical" German is a model of robotlike obedience to his superiors, while a "typical" Frenchman of the same period is much too individualistic for such submissive conduct. No sixteenth-century observer would have recognized his German and French contemporaries by such descriptions. Here are Emperor Maximilian's reported thoughts on the two peoples: He, the emperor, king of kings, was obeyed by no one, while the French king ruled over a herd of sheep.[1] And Maximilian's successor, Charles V, warned the German Protestants, who had allied themselves in the name of German liberty with the French king, that they would find little liberty in France, certainly not as Protestants, and not even as ordinary citizens under a king who owned everything in his realm.[2] Machiavelli[3] as well as the Venetian ambassadors[4] marveled at the French people's obedience and reverence for their king. The English ambassador could write to his king as late as 1609 that the French king [Henry IV] "by simple edict or proclamation... may make what levies... he pleaseth."[5] In the realm of culture, the polished company of Castiglione's *Cortigiano*

agreed that France "abhorred" fine letters, although the incoming king, Francis I, was expected to improve matters considerably.[6] Erasmus, who had a bad word for virtually everybody, said, among other things, that the French were intellectually sluggish.[7] Paris too, it would seem, has changed greatly since the sixteenth century,[7a] when it was a citadel of ultraconservatism, leading the country, as in many other matters, in the extermination of Protestants in 1572. If Paris erected barricades as efficiently then as at later dates, those of 1588 were constructed to repulse unorthodoxy along with all danger of compromise with rebels. The prose style of the sixteenth century differed strongly from what has for many generations been considered the essence of French genius: measure, lucidity, discipline. Overflowing with erudition, quotations, and digressions, the prose advanced by association of thought rather than through the agency of a guiding idea, or, for that matter, of a given title.[8]

National character is, certainly, another elusive matter.[9] What may impress a contemporary, whether native or foreign, as characteristic is usually contingent, and usually only one aspect of a great number of features. On the other hand, those qualities that are not ephemeral are likely not to be particular to a country. Royalism assuredly has been a pronounced characteristic of French history.[10] Yet glorification, even deification, of the sovereign was as pronounced in all other European countries united under a king.[11] Would national consciousness perhaps be more indigenous to the people responsible for introducing the word chauvinism? Some French and non-French authors were convinced of it. Barrès, for one, wrote: "We are the nation that, first in Europe, had the idea of forming one fatherland."[12] Hanotaux (politician, historian) wrote that the feeling of belonging to a fatherland "appears with us at a time when most other peoples are still blinded by the dust of internal dissensions."[13] An extensive list of events and sayings would serve to confirm the "Frenchness" of the concept: from the "sweet France" of the *Chanson de Roland* through Jeanne d'Arc's patriotic deeds, the awe-inspiring glory that resided at Versailles for more than fifty years, the "Day of Glory" which had arrived in 1792, the Napoleonic epic, and down to our own days, when, regardless of weakness and degradation, the ancient glory was once again flung, as defiantly as ever, in the face of an all too neglectful world.

Since, however, no country in Europe was remiss in flaunting its own excellence, perhaps France merely had more style when attempting to impress friend and foe.[14] Exhibitions of superiority, here too, were only partly the natural expression of self-confidence. They were also a means of compensating for failures, for France was not only different from the France of our time, she was far from being what she would become even 100 years later. There were still many things that eluded her. The important inventions—gunpowder and the printing press—were made elsewhere. Her Spanish rival had enlarged its lands and augmented its power immeasurably through exploitation of the New World. And Spain had achieved, long before France, religious uniformity. As for England, she had in times not long past inflicted searing defeats on France, and these on French soil. England held Calais until 1558, occupied Le Harve in the period 1562-1564, and supported—morally more than financially—the French Protestants. With imperial Germany, France found herself, at least as far as status was concerned, at a disadvantage.[15] And finally there was Italy. All military undertakings here were to end in failure, but well before, Italian superiority in cultural matters, combined with actual and imagined condescension, had provoked the same ugly reactions in France as elsewhere. The humanists were, of course, the last to deny Italy its famous status as true descendent of ancient Rome, instructress in all mundane arts, and object of pilgrimage for worshippers of antiquity. Yet, by the same token, as the French students increased their own abilities and their own contributions to the revival of letters, as they learned to look into, and admire, their own past, they began to notice that Italy was weak, both militarily and politically. Good Christians had also learned to despise Rome as the seat of a sinful papacy. In addition, Italy became the birthplace of Machiavelli, the incarnation of immorality, and during the French civil wars, also of Machiavelli's "spiritual daughter," the Queen Mother, Catherine of Medici.[16] Xenophobia was aroused by the presence of the many Italian merchants, financiers, and civil servants who held influential and well-remunerated positions in France.[17] Forty years of civil wars were not only weakening the moral fiber of the country but were also detrimental to its image. And yet, by the seventeenth century, the "eternal" character of France was entirely transformed; she had overtaken Italy and Spain and had left civil wars to England and Germany.

Back in the sixteenth century, two humanist disputes palpably demonstrated nationalistic motivations. One was an "epistolary duel" between the physician-humanist Symphorien Champier (1471-1535) and a learned canonist from Asti, Jerome of Pavia. The correspondence was published in 1519.[18] Champier assumed that the Italian would be flattered to be termed a "Roman Gaul." In his letter he indulged himself with praises of the splendors, of the fabulous origin, of the degree of learning in his native Lyon and the rest of France. Jerome, resenting the appellation, refuted Champier's presumptions point by point, finally declaring that France would have to go far before equaling Italy in the language of Cicero. In the same year, 1519, an oratorical disputation in Rome led to a confrontation of Christophle Longueil (1488-1522), a protégé of Budé, with the Roman intelligentsia. Longueil was to be honored with Roman citizenship, but before it could be conferred, it became known that, eleven years earlier, in a speech in Poitiers, he had proclaimed France's superiority over Italy in arms, religion, and erudition.[19] Opposition to granting this man citizenship became bitter, and Longueil was forced to respond with a long explanation in which he touted Rome as exuberantly as he had once praised France. The citizenship was finally granted, but Longueil left Rome and never returned.

In Guillaume Budé (1468-1540), national feelings certainly stemmed from motives nobler than common vanity.

He sought peace for himself and his equals in their erudite pursuits and approached the problem by supporting absolute authority for their king, who would, he hoped, respond by attending to the scientists' needs and supporting their ambitions for France. He requested from the powerful enlightened interest in erudition, and he pressed for a seat of classical learning, independent of the antiquated and meddlesome Sorbonne,[20] a seat urgently needed to compete with centers already existing outside of France: Louvain, in the Netherlands, Alcalà, in Spain, as well as the many city universities in Italy. Budé's ambition and his impatience with the slow progress of the academy promised by Francis I explain to a good degree his changing moods toward his countrymen, which he expressed by alternately scolding and praising them. Complaints about the ignorance and indifference of the courtiers who should have furthered eloquence but did not are followed by assurances that French minds were as capable as any others of shining in classical languages.[22] We may misread the correspondence of the humanists. They knew, no doubt, what was written to impress fellow classicists and posterity, and what was sober information. But possibly a letter from Budé offering Erasmus the directorship of the future Collège des lecteurs royaux sounded as bombastic to him as it does to us: he advertises the French king as "the greatest and most illustrious" and impresses upon an Erasmus "what honor it will be for you, how splendid and fortunate it will seem to all other erudites that you have been invited . . . on the recommendation of your learning alone."[22a] And it is not impossible that such patriotic vanities, added to other reasons, might have been the deciding element in Erasmus' refusal of the post.[23]

We find a good number of nationalistic expressions in the Erasmus-Budé correspondence.[24] that could easily be compared to other proud voices in France.[24a] An entirely different, original note sounds in the preface of Budé's *De Asse*. He explains that this work is dedicated not "to any individual but to the French genius and to the fatherland," that he seeks no reward other than the gratitude of France and of Paris. He then returns to his deep grievance, namely that the opinion still prevailed that the French mind was by nature banished from Minerva's company. He believes that with the present work he has disproved the absurd bias.[25] When sending a later edition to the king, he again writes that he hopes to have demonstrated "the excellence of the French nation.... the magnificence of your... kingdom... and it is for this reason that I have dedicated the book to the honor and fortune of France and her guardian angel, and to the majesty of your noble kingdom, to increase your empire and kingdom, into which I was born, as were my children and my ancestors too.[26] These were not ready-made panegyrics for king, God, or even erudition. Budé's mind at that moment had visibly fastened on the nation, while the king appeared dimly behind such abstractions as majesty, crown, kingdom, and even that only in the edition he had dedicated to the king himself.

Etienne Dolet (1509-1546), perhaps influenced by Budé, addressed his *Manière de bien traduire* to the French people. In contrast to Budé, however, Dolet wrote in French rather than in Latin, saying: "Etienne Dolet to the French people, humble salutation and wishes for increased honor and power.... To glorify you by all means I composed this work in our language.... Adieu, people most triumphant in the world, in virtue as well as in power."[27]

That the king also knew how to make the right gesture toward his country is evidenced, for example, when Francis addressed the troops before the battle of Marignan in 1515. He assured them that their prince would not be ungrateful for their bravery, for the "services rendered to me and to the whole French kingdom."[28] Dolet places the speech after the victory over the Swiss and has the king say: "Companions, the French nation has triumphed over her enemies. She will not be daunted by arms." And Francis ironically adds: "Ah, aren't the Swiss just the people to defeat the French nation and the king of the French."[29] The French king had to flatter his subjects; it was as much his duty as it was that of the German emperor (see pp. 47 ff.).

But the vanity of a nation could best be enhanced in history writing. History told of a brave past and, above all, of a famous ancestry in which the highest and the lowest members of society had equally shared. A race might descend from no other people (as the Germans claimed for themselves), springing up autochthonously, or it might stem from a noble ancient house: from Noah, Hector, Hercules, or some son of theirs. The royal line in Gallic France had begun, tradition taught, in A.D. 420 with King Pharamond.[30] All these "historical" romances were composed for national gratification, against rival claims and also certainly for solace in depressing times.

Hotman (1524-1590) called the Trojan saga material for poets, not for historians.[31] Pasquier (1529-1615) seemed not altogether sure whether to reject it, but drily wondered what honor France could possibly derive from an ancestor who had to flee his conquered homeland.[32] The historian Du Tillet (d. 1570) established in the first sentence of his *Recueil* that the Germanic Franks were the ancestors of today's Frenchmen, and he thought it infinitely more reputable to descend from intrepid, unvanquished Germans than from imaginary Trojans, whose claim to fame was their ultimate ruin.[33] But Germanic parentage was not a quality French patriots valued very highly. François Connan (1508-1551) denied that the Franks had come from Germany: Gaul was their homeland. They were at one time forced to emigrate, settling in Germany, but they had returned to Gaul as soon as times were again pacific.[34] In the last chapter of his *Méthode,* Jean Bodin (1530-1596) went to tortuous lengths to prove that the Gauls, or Celts, or Franks, did not originate in Germany but had merely crossed the Rhine into Germany, remaining for a period, then returning to Gaul.[35] Du Haillan (1535-1610) gives the same version.[36] Pasquier had set out to investigate the French past in order to show its excellence; the Gauls had, unforgivably, neglected to broadcast their own deeds, "so great was our [forebears'] zeal to act rightly, not to write down their deeds."[37] Another means of establishing an aristocratic stock lay in claiming a Greek relationship with France. Bodin, in the same last chapter of the *Méthode,* says that "the ancient Celtic language was for the most part Greek, because our ancestors are derived from that people." His etymology is quite creaky, but he was not alone in maintaining a "Celto-Greek" tie.[38] Five years earlier, Joachim Périon (1499-1559), for one, had unhesitatingly written that "our Gallic tongue partly originated in Greek," and in four dialogues he proved a close relation between the two languages.[39] Pasquier did not believe in any Greek origin of race or language;[40] he had accumulated his material to illuminate the high level of Gallic civilization achieved without aid from Rome or Athens. For other Frenchmen, however, it was not enough to be related to ancient Greece; they had to demonstrate that the Gauls were responsible for bringing civilization to Greece.

It is a simple matter to dismiss propagandists of ancient Gaul like Jean Picard, of whom not much is known, who wrote ten books in Latin on Celtic culture,[41] or like Le Fèvre de la Boderie (1541-1598), who combined patriotism with cabalism in his *Galliad.*[42] All times have their eccentrics, and printing presses must be kept busy. But how does the celebrated dialectician, mathematician, philosopher, Ramus, fit into this crowd? Ramus (1515-1572) wrote a *Book on the Ancient Gauls' Customs*[43] in which, on page 74, he asserted that what Caesar had taken to be Greek letters found on Gallic soil, he, Ramus, called Gallic letters. They had not come to Gaul from Greece; rather the Gauls had taken them to Greece. Gallic culture flourished long before Cadmus arrived in Greece [to introduce the alphabet], and there could be no doubt that the Gauls had a written language centuries before the Greeks. Ramus had occasion to express his patriotism in a more serious manner. He refused an offer to teach in Bologna because, he wrote, "I am a Frenchman, and my King's liberality has supported me and my studies for many years. I owe myself entirely first of all to my country, then to my King."[44] This sense of priorities should be noted, as should the thought of gratitude toward one's country.

The urge to refurbish the past, to illuminate the dim

outlines of the country's beginnings, resulted, as far as the author's conscience permitted, in suppression of information about the two quasi-total conquests of Gaul: the absorption by the Romans, and then by the Germanic tribes. That effort is reflected in the French insistence in referring to themselves as Gauls or as Celts.[45] To explain the appellation of France, a benevolent legend had offered a founder of Priam's house, Francus or Francion, whom Ronsard, as we know, also gratefully adopted.[46] The French Church underscored her emancipation from the Roman yoke by calling herself the Gallic Church that defended Gallic liberties.[47] In 1594 Pierre Pithou (1539-1596) published his *Libertés de l'Eglise gallicane,*[48] and the same year marked the composition, though not publication, of a work by Guy Coquille (1523-1603), a *Traité des libertés de l'Eglise de France.*[49] No less devoted to France than Pithou, Coquille was yet generous enough to allow that the Franks had come to Gaul from Saxony, and that their king, Hugh Capet, was of the race of those who had conquered Gaul. The word "France" was not really shunned, but the prevalence of the Gallomania, Celtomania, and Greco-Gallomania surely suggests a determination to refuse any room in French history to Germans, Romans, and the latter's descendents, Italians.[49a]

The modern reader occasionally has a sensation of a déjà vu in reverse when observing the vitriolic polemics of a Henri Estienne (1531?-1598) against Italians and Italizanized Frenchmen. The terror that seized post-World War II France, that fear of becoming Americanized, of being robbed of her substance, of having to watch her language bastardized, we find it all in sixteenth-century France's attitude toward Italy; witness Estienne's persistant censures, warnings, and lamentations about his country's demoralized ways.[50] The outcries, then as today, came too late. The dreaded habits had been successfully transplanted and without visible harm to the receivers. It may be argued that the stridency and injustice of the denigrations were in proportion to the obvious benefits France had derived from her foreign models. For, given native talent, a devouring ambition to be unsurpassed in any aspect of life and thought can act as a powerful stimulus.

Estienne, then, published his first French work in 1565, the *Conformité du language françois avec le grec.* His thesis was that of all languages, Greek was the finest, that French resembled it in roots and forms, and therefore French was, of all modern language, the most excellent. A list of words and expressions to prove his point followed. In the preface, he says that he is "a true Frenchman, born in the heart of France [Paris], and so the more jealous of his country's honor."[51] He expressed himself similarly fourteen years later in a dedication to Henry III of his *Précellence du language françois.* His heart, he wrote, was always jealous of his nation's honor, and his father and his uncle had also had an ardent love for their country, so that the feeling had become hereditary, and he would not know how to uproot it.[52]

Estienne represents the many propagandists for a better French language, which they intended to render illustrious.[53] To have labored for the glory of France became, as it were, a consecrated formula for prefaces and dedications of French-written books. Under the pen of many a humanist such a claim achieved a certain ambiguity, for we realize how deeply all of them, in all countries, were drenched in antiquity-worship. The mother tongue had no place at all in their education and thinking, and the sudden dedication to the vernacular could not but have been a wrenching experience. To immerse oneself in Greek and Latin, leaving the national language to peasants and women, was not a natural law, royal ordinance, or popular demand. The articulate, knowledgable clique itself had first overvalued antiquity and then impressed its values upon the consciousness of the more and less educated and their faithful followers. Certainly, they had not created the problem without collaboration or antecedent. Fauchet (1530-1601) accused the Church of having prevented the normal development of all vernaculars. In the worldwide net of Church business and interests, he charged, whoever wanted to advance himself in life had to deal with the Church, and that meant studying Latin.[54] In our time, Brunot[55] and Chamard[56] found additional culprits in universities and in the wave of neo-Latin poets. Yet, no Church and no university can induce a poet who has a living language at his disposal to write in Latin, unless he wishes to use that idiom. We can imagine various reasons for poets and erudites to plunge headlong into the ancient world, even if we leave aside the practical point of the internationality of Latin. Here and there, it might have represented a flight from the present. Some writers, perhaps, sought to explore new sounds and associations. Perhaps the very difficulty of writing poetry, if not prose, in Latin accounted for some of its attraction.[57] And there was, in addition, always the status accorded to Latinists.

The problem of this kind of linguistic schizophrenia must have prevailed in all European countries that had allowed Latin to dispossess for too long the natural language: for while their ambiance was the vernacular, their intellectual center, their training, pride, faith, and measure had become anchored in the ancient world. Thus, we read in practically all linguistic discussions the argument that the mother tongue was, regrettably, not yet rich enough, that it would continue to have to borrow from the old models for a while. The truth was—and the fact was not overlooked at the time—that no one saw to the culture of the native tongue, while the schools forced Latin upon their pupils. The writer's difficulty in breaking the hold of the ancient languages is understandable.

Nonetheless, the fashion was changing; it was time to let go, at least to some extent, of an artificial world. And so the humanists scrambled to be seen in the service of the mother tongue. Translators never forgot to explain what had made them leave their usual milieu. They never failed "to exalt ostentatiously the new conquest by which they have enriched France." and sometimes they even neglected to give due credit to the translated author. (So remarked Blignières, a century ago, in his biography of the famous translator Amyot.)[58] Dolet's patriotic preface to a method of translation has been mentioned previously (p. 62). In a dedicatory letter to the work, he explained to those who might be surprised to find so inveterate a Latinist now writing in French that he intended to further the French language. Addressing the "French people," he promised to make the language illustrious by all means at his disposal.[59] When Amyot (1513-1593) offered Henry II his translation of Plutarch, he humbly requested the king to continue on his father's glorious path "receiving [as had his father] in his noble kingdom fine letters that daily embellished our language, so that neither Italian, Spanish, or any other idiom can compete with it."[60] Belleforest (1530-1583), continuing a translation begun by Dolet of letters by famous Romans, urged more and more translations into French. These would show all foreigners that any and every science can be treated in French, which was "today so finely honed that it needs nothing whatsoever from other languages."[61] Another noted translator, Louis Le Roy (1510?-1577), chose another forum to recommend the "natural" language. In 1576 he gave two speeches in French at the Royal College, where the use of the vernacular was not customary. He scolded those who felt at home in Athens, Carthage, or Parthia, and who stubbornly studied ancient languages, remaining completely ignorant of current affairs. They would do better to devote themselves to the language "used today among men and to know affairs of the present time."[62]

The manifesto urging the defense and illustration of French that made literary history, appeared right in the middle of the century. Du Bellay's *Défense et Illustration de la langue française* of 1549 also stands between the two opposing tendencies; it propagandizes the use of French and, at the same time, recommends ever deeper to explore the classical languages. To appropriate the devices of the ancients and to graft them onto French seemed to the defenders the only right and patriotic method toward a better, richer French. The stance, incidentally, left them in the enviable position of being able to worship at two altars. The French-praising and French-writing humanist felt doubly praiseworthy. But the Latin-writing poets labored no less for their country's honor.[63]

Salmon Macrin (1490-1557), for one, addressed a poem to the Latin-writing Gallic poets, praising them for the efforts which had raised Gallic poets to a level that could no longer be called barbaric. No longer were they inferior to the Italians.[64] Chamard[65] and Murarasu[66] believe that the "neo"-French authors considered the neo-Latinists as rivals and that that feeling raised the formers' propagandistic pitch. Perhaps this was so. Yet the noisy vows to nurture a worthier French must also have concealed the uncertainties implied in a new mentality, a mentality that could almost be called a new ideology.

In any event, the patriotic tone found room in both Latin and vernacular writing with equal aplomb. "France, mother of arts, of arms, and of laws.... I fill caverns and woods with your name," sang Du Bellay (*Regrets* IX). He vowed that he would no longer look into Greek books, that he did not want to revive dead monuments (*Regrets* IV), and in the *Défence* (p. 319), we read that "the same law that commands one to defend the place of his birth obliges us also to keep up the dignity of our language." It would be laboring the obvious to summon up Du Bellay's or Ronsard's patriotic manifestations.[67] One example might show how Ronsard dealt with the problem of training and early preference, on the one hand, and of patriotism, or opportunism, on the other. In the posthumous edition of his works there exists a new preface to the *Franciade*. It is quite long and is, more than anything else, a manual addressed to the "Apprentice Reader," whom he wants to instruct in the appreciation and composition of a successful French epic. The pages are filled with Latin quotations, the advice given based exclusively on Greek and Latin examples. Then Ronsard turns to the question of language. He counsels the student to learn to perfection Latin, Greek, Italian, and Spanish. After that "withdraw, like a good soldier, under your own flag and compose in your maternal language, as did Homer" and many other classics. "For it is a crime of high treason to abandon the language of one's own country.... in order to unearth God knows what ancient ashes, and to yelp about the high spirits of the dead."[68] Du Bellay's and Ronsard's exhortations to let dead ashes and old monuments alone was sage advice, but did it come naturally to the commanders of so many golddiggers in ancient ashes, to the admired hunters (Ronsard, in particular) after high spirits of the dead?[69]

Around 1542, an anonymous poet had collected in verse form all the arguments of the defenders of the mother tongue, chiding the French for neglect, urging instruction in their language for every man, woman, and child in the land, and that early in life, while the twig was green, before wasting precious years learning dead languages. The native language ought to be cultivated, so that its fame would spread over the whole world and every nation would want to learn it. The king would be swept to the heights of power on the wave of this glory (we hear Nebrija again), to become a monarch whom all kings would gladly serve. The task before the French was to teach their language to all Frenchmen in all subjects.[70]

One last voice must be heard on that matter of Latin versus French, a voice outstanding for its intelligence, common sense, avoidance of rhetoric, and, above all, for the fact that the author practiced what he preached. In 1552, Estienne Pasquier wrote in a letter to Adrien Turnèbe (1512-1565) that he was not of Turnèbe's opinion that serious matters had to be written in Latin. The entire reply is worth reading, as it explains, in its zigzag manner, with quiet pride, what French could do, had already done. Pasquier said that things had changed so much since Roman times that the Roman vocabulary was no longer appropriate to modern needs. The prejudice in favor of Latin was worldwide because so much fame could be won through its use. Latin was possibly richer than French, but then it was intended for different, more public purposes than French. We must, of course, study dead languages to comprehend the ancients' philosophies. But as far as the poverty of the French tongue was concerned, Pasquier would like Turnèbe to show him in what field it could not express all it wanted and that in a variety of ways: "At no time our language was indigent, but we treat it as the miser does with his treasure, we hide it, instead of putting it to work." Greeks and Romans wrote in their own languages. "We alone have remained stuck in that superstitious ingratitude communicating among us only in terms that nobody understands without interpreter. . . . I cannot imagine that the Greeks would have produced great philosophers if they had studied in Chaldean or Egyptian. . . . Let us encourage those who are capable of beginning the good work. In a short while, our language will cross the Pyrenees, the Alps, and the Rhine."[71]

We may well wonder with Pasquier in what way the language was wanting, considering the verbal acrobatics of a Rablais, considering the subtleties that a Montaigne was able to formulate, considering the quantity of sixteenth-century poetry that was produced throughout France. The people whose centuries-old catch phrase had been "One King, One Faith, One Law" could legitimately have added "One Language, French."[72]

Queen Elizabeth I of England, engraving by Crispin de Passe.

England

This royal throne of Kings, this sceptr'd isle,
This earth of majesty, this seat of Mars,
This other Eden, demi-paradise;
This fortress built by nature for herself,
Against infection and the hand of war;
This happy breed of men, this little world;
This precious stone set in the Silver sea,
Which serves it in the office of a wall,
Or as a moat defensive to a house,
Against the envy of less happier lands;
This blessed plot, this earth, this realm, this England,
This nurse, this teeming womb of royal kings,
Fear'd by their breed, and famous by their birth,
Renowned for their deeds as far from home,
For Christian service and true chivalry,
As is the sepulchre in stubborn Jewry
Of the world's ransom, blessed Mary's son;
This land of such dear souls, this dear, dear land,
Dear for her reputation through the world....
England, bound in with the triumphant sea,
Whose rocky shore beats back the envious siege
Of wat'ry Neptune....

> Shakespeare, *Richard II*, act 2, scene 1[1]

It is true that, for such magnificence of expression, England had to await the 1590s. But the thought, the sentiment of the speech was common property of the country as it was, manifestly, of the whole age. If English praise of all things English was distinguishable from self-adulation on the continent, it was only in its narrower compass, in its almost

73

exclusive interest in state and religion—in the religious state, in the state religion—and in England's special relation with God himself. One imagines that patriotic declarations in the first half of the century, given England's internal turmoil, must have been more nervous and defiant, more braggadocio than confidence. The second half-century, a time that was to become one of the country's great periods, naturally gave patriots material enough to demonstrate their worth. Under Henry VIII (reigned 1509-1547), England was no worse off than the rest of Europe: there was bloody cruelty everywhere, but at least she was not drawn into the Habsburg-Valois wars. Yet there was a foreign, hostile land, Scotland, with which England shared her own island, a playground for blunt and effective French intervention, a constant danger and a powerful occasion for xenophobia, if not direct and cold-blooded intervention.[2]

When dealing politically, commercially, or intellectually with Europe, Henry's England could see how far behind she lagged in most fields. England was poorer in population, in flourishing cities, in most skills, in cultural achievements.[3] The best-intentioned observer must have felt uneasy at the King's satraplike behavior, his evenhanded arbitrariness with wives, daughters, devoted counselors, and the country's most celebrated men, be they Catholic or Protestant. But when Henry jerked England out of her traditional religious loyalty, he no doubt created the central event of his reign. It was not done in one clean cut, rather only after years of changing politics, each swing felling martyrs right and left, victims of the King's vacillating policies. Englishmen and the rest of Europe wondered how Catholic powers would react to the break with Rome, and Protestants to the burning of Lutherans in England. But, as we know, lucky circumstances allowed Henry to become the head of his national Church without internal or international catastrophe. His people had, at the very least, the satisfaction of having exchanged a foreign pope for a domestic one, their own rightful King.[4]

The English humanists meanwhile had been caught by

the fashion and passion of the time, the search for their racial origin. Each nation, it would seem, strove to dig itself out from under the international blanket of Christian brotherhood. Each nation strove to prove to itself, and to the world at large, its distinctive prowess and the many virtues it had inherited from its fabled beginnings. English antiquaries, like their colleagues elsewhere, wandered across the country in search of ancient vestiges, while historians looked into neglected documents and chronicles and published their factual or legendary findings. The English chronicler, R. Fabyan (d. 1513), tells us in a rhymed "Prologus" that he had not toiled for glory or money but "of course only for that I would spread / The famous honor of this fertile land."[5] England's first important archeologist-antiquary, John Leland (1506?-1552), traveled some nine years throughout Britain noting down localities, monuments, inscriptions, and coins, and thus accumulated an immense collection of raw material, which was put to good use by generations of patriotic historians. John Bale (1495-1563) published a treasury of old-English authors out of Leland's manuscripts. Shortly thereafter, he dedicated to the new king, Edward VI, a small work in which he explained the worth and range of Leland's diligence. He used Leland's words to present a point, then he took over and commented on the same subject, then quoted Leland again, fortifying the position in his own words, and so forth. The work is part lamentation about the long neglect of England's past, part praise of the country's accomplishments. Leland, for instance, had collected old authors and had shown "that there is no kind of liberal science, or any feat concerning learning, in which they have not shown certain arguments of great felicity of wit." "I trust," Bale said of the effect of Leland's journeys around the island, "that so to open this window... the light shall be seen... by the space of a whole thousand years stopped up, and the old glory of your renowned Britain to reflourish." And, he added, the king will see in a few years that "this your realm be so well known, once painted with his native colors, that the renommé thereof shall give place to the glory of no other region." A few pages later, Bale wrote that Leland's "hope as mine is . . . that these things once done, England which has of the Italians and Frenchmen been reckoned a barbarous nation, their monuments aforetime not known, will appear from thence forth, equal with the proudest of them, and in all kinds of learning."[6] We see the same yearning as elsewhere for recognition by others, and the same prodding of those in power to sustain and further the burning desire of the learned elite to distinguish the nation by their contributions.

Equally all-European was the persuasion of a noble descent. There were the English Trojan partisans—those who held for the eponymic Brutus, great-grandson of Aeneas—and there were those who argued against more enlightened historians for the existence of King Arthur.[7] Fables found entrance into politics and diplomacy. For instance, in 1531 Henry's representative, the Duke of Norfolk, conferred with Charles V's ambassador, Eustache Chapuys, and impressed upon Chapuys the ancient imperial sovereignty of English kings and the illegality of the pope's claim to British obedience. The Duke's arguments reached far back into Roman times, when, according to English chronicles, Brennus, "an Englishman" (!) had conquered Rome, and when Constantine, "whose mother was English, reigned here."[8] Imperial rights had, therefore, come down to English kings in direct succession from the "English" Emperor Constantine.[9] In the course of the same conversation, Norfolk also informed Chapuys of King Arthur's role in England's imperial history. Chapuys was not sure how to answer these absurdities, while we may explain them as sheer exasperation on Henry's part in his struggle for a divorce and freedom from Rome. Neither he nor Norfolk could possibly have believed their own arguments; yet such myths were part of sixteenth-century history writing. In the same spirit antiquarians discovered the truth about Britain's Christianization. She had not received the Gospel from Roman missionaries but, rather, directly from one of the apostles. Philip had sent Joseph of Arimathias with twelve companions to convert the island, and this was long before

there had been popes in Rome.[10] England's complete
independence had to be assured in the religious realm too.

Altogether, much had happened on the national scene
during Henry's reign to gratify the national sentiment, and,
almost incidentally, also to advance the cause of the
Protestants. Henry had removed the obstacles that elsewhere
impeded the progress of religious reformers. The spiritual seat
of English Catholicism had been transferred from Rome to
Canterbury. Church duties and donations remained in Britain.
And with the dissolution of all religious centers and orders, the
pope had no foothold left in English soil. The king had also
encouraged the search for national monuments, from which
the antiquarians had produced evidence of Britain's long and
valorous past, her imperial lineage, her native Christianity.
Independence in the entire religio-political field had been
declared, and, at the very least, these achievements compensat-
ed for present-day discomfort.

In the entanglement of religion and politics, it turned
out that religion, in its specifically English form of Christianity, profited most from the dramatic reversals of politics.
Reformers—Protestants or Puritans—practically monopo-
lized the national spirit. Obedience to the supreme head of the
country was part of the Protestant doctrine, and they preached
it from the altar and in pamphlets and books.[11] Maintenance of
the dynasty was part of everybody's faith,[12] but xenophobia,
too, helped the Protestant cause.[13] Under the Tudors,
xenophobia was exacerbated by the persons of Mary, Queen of
Scots, and of Mary Tudor. The Scottish Mary—a despised
foreigner—was Catholic, and, through family ties, marriage,
and upbringing, she was practically French as well. The danger
that she represented to the succession to the English throne
remained a problem until her end.[14] The other Mary's marriage
to Spain's Philip II increased England's fear of being
swallowed by the most powerful of the Catholic nations.[15] In
both cases, the anti-Catholics would clearly be the better
Englishmen in the eyes of public opinion. It is also in
Protestant writings that we find the expressions "God's

Englishmen," "English God," or "God's Elect Nation" for England. Religion and politics, England and God, it all became a biblically guaranteed union and uniqueness that culminated in Elizabeth's "happy reign."

In 1539, one of Henry's humanist apologists, Richard Morison (d. 1556), wrote *An Exhortation to Stir All Englishmen to the Defense of Their Country,* intended to rally England behind the king, to ward off the French by reminding them of past English victories over them, and to strike another blow at the pope. Toward the end of the *Exhortation* he wrote: "Why may we not think that the noble Henry VIII is the lion... sent by God to toss this wicked tyrant of Rome, to blow him out of all Christian regions? See you not to what honor God calls our nation? May not we rejoice that God has chosen our king, to work so noble a feat?.... Let us fight this one field with English hands and English hearts...."[16]

When Henry's son, Edward, was born in 1537, Latimer (1485?-1555), the Bishop of Worcester, preacher, and martyr for his religion under the next reign, wrote to Henry's Chancellor, Thomas Cromwell (1485?-1540): "... Here is no less rejoicing... for the birth of our prince, whom we hungered so long, than there was... at the birth of St. John Baptist-.... thanks to our Lord God, God of England! for verily he has shown himself God of England, or rather an English God...."[17] Years later, Latimer preached before Edward, now King, and, apparently still echoing the general relief at the smooth—and legitimate—succession to the throne, he said at one point: "It has pleased God to grant us a natural liege King and lord of our own nation, an Englishman, one of our own religion... a most precious treasure.... Oh, what a plague were it, that a strange King, of a strange land, and of a strange religion, should reign over us!"[18] The young king died in 1553. He had, said Elton, "the inhuman passion of an adolescent indoctrinated [in Protestantism] since childhood."[19] And on his deathbed Edward is reported to have prayed: "Oh my Lord, bless Thy people, and save Thine inheritance. O Lord God, save Thy chosen people of England."[20]

For minds trained to think in associations and parallels with antique models—Christian or pagan—it was quite natural to identify those persecuted and exiled under Queen Mary with the earliest Christian victims of cruel rulers. Once again, God-chosen people suffered God-willed trials as witnesses of their faith.[21] While the Marian martyrs died in England, their ordeals and their outstanding courage were recorded by the exiles, among whom the most influential voice was that of John Foxe (1517-1587).[22] Foxe might well have intended his chronicle of Christian martyrs to be universal, but the role he attributed to the English in the whole of Christian history, and the description of the sufferings of his Protestant brothers endured at the moment, gave to his work a pro-English, anti-Spanish, and, naturally, anti-Roman thrust.[23]

The reign of the unfortunate Queen Mary came to an end after five and a half years, and under the "new Constantine" we hear still more of God's special interest in Englishmen.[24] Aylmer (1521-1594), future Bishop of London, replied in 1559 to Knox's *Trumpet Blast against the Monstruous Regiment of Women*. Aylmer's *Harborowe for Faithful...Subjects* was a defense of women, of the new Queen, and of England, in general. Comparing England most favorably with other countries, he exhorted his countrymen to thank God for having made them English "and not French peasants, nor an Italian, nor Aleman."[25] God was on their side, "for you fight not only in the quarrel of your country but also... in the defense of his true religion." And in the margin of this passage were printed the words "God is English."[26] Or the Archbishop of Canterbury, Matthew Parker (1504-1575), in a letter to the Lord Treasurer, Burghley, wrote "Where Almighty God is so much English as he is, should not we requite his mercy?"[27] Or John Lyly (1554?-1606), in his *Euphues and His England,* of 1580, spoke of God's mercy, "So tender a care has He always had of that England as of a new Israel, his chosen and peculiar people";[28] and a few pages further on: "O blessed peace, O happy prince, O fortunate people! The living God is only the English God, where He has placed peace.... This peace has the Lord continued with great and unspeakable goodness among his chosen people of England."[29] And there is the example of Job Throckmorton (1545-1601), parliamentarian and pamphleteer, who, in the 1587 Parliament, expressed his boundless gratitude to God for his gift of a queen such as Elizabeth: "We that have lived in the eyes of all men so choked... with blessings of God beyond desert, we... confess that indeed the Lord has vowed himself to be English."[30] We discern the closeness that merchants and explorers seemed to feel to a native God when we read that one of them, Edward Hayes, affirmed that newly discovered "countries lying north of Florida, God has reserved... to be reduced unto Christian civility by the English nation."[31] As for the next example, it is unlikely that a later, more officially "imperialistic" period in English history could surpass it in combining national self-assurance, science and trade interests, and trust in God and Bible. The explorer John Davys (1550?-1605) recommended assiduous explorations of all parts of the world, to discover and to measure seas and lands, "since it is so appointed that there shall be one shepherd and one flock, what hinders us of England... to attempt that which God himself has appointed to be performed? There is no doubt but that we of England are his saved people, by the eternal and infallible presence of the Lord predestined to be sent unto these Gentiles in the sea, to those isles and kingdoms, there to preach the peace of the Lord, for are not we only set upon Mount Zion to give light to all the rest of the world?... By whom then shall the truth be preached but by them unto whom the truth shall be revealed? It is only we, therefore, that must be these shining messengers of the Lord, and none but we."[32]

Self-congratulation, when accompanied by denigration of others, is more effective. So, in his *Harborowe,* Aylmer slapped Italians and Frenchmen, saying that "England is the paradise and not Italy, as commonly they call it" (folio P. 4*r*). Yes, the Italians did have fruits that England had not, but then England had riches, "which they lack." As for the French, they were miscreants, allies of the Turks, "the enemies of Christ" (fols. Qv-Q 2v), and they are very rightly afraid of Englishmen. England has the Truth, for "Wycliffe begat Huss, Huss begat Luther, Luther begat truth" (fol. Rv).

In *The Description of England,* by W. Harrison (1534-1593) published between the years 1577 and 1587, there are not infrequent rebukes of England, but the all-encompassing work is full of self-conscious comparisons with other countries, always to the advantage of the author's home country. Whether he disapproved of English students or sons of English gentlemen traveling to Italy, whence they could only return as morally damaged atheists or cynics;[33] whether he declared that English corpses preserved their forms longer, and that English women over forty were handsomer than their French counterparts;[34] or, finally, whether he attributed English courage to the northern climate, and noted that Southerners were feeble but crafty,[35] the result was always a propagandistic undertaking that might have raised English spirits. It could not have convinced foreigners who had their own propaganda. Lyly's *Euphues and His England* swept over the entire island, and the only fault he could see in his countrymen was their delusion that everything was better abroad. He set them right, exclaiming, "O thrice happy England.... where such people live, where such virtue springeth!"[36] But he had, shortly before, already quoted an epigram to the effect that "All countries stand in need of Britain, and Britain of none."[37] Infinitely more discreet and noble sound Camden's (1551-1623) words, as he dedicated his Latin *Britannia* to Burghley, and then addressed the Reader. To Burghley he declared that the difficulty of the undertaking would have deterred him, but his country's fame gave him the impulse to attack the work. He dreaded the burden but could not contemplate failing his country. He would frankly admit, he then informed the Benevolent Reader, that love of fatherland, glory of Britain's name, and his friends' entreaties combined to overcome his reluctance. "Your kindness, good reader, my diligence, love of fatherland, Britain's noble name, may they come to my aid."[38] It was humanistic diction, but there is no substantial difference in saying *patria* rather than fatherland, *gloria* instead of fame. Camden understood, without childish vainglory, the worth and singularity of England, as he prepared to furnish the English part of an international attempt at geographical and historical reconstruction of the Roman Empire.[39]

It simply will not do to maintain that the sixteenth century knew nationalism only in the form of loyalty to one's prince, or, alternatively, to one's province. The following brief reminders should prove the contrary.

Item: The leader of a 1536 rebellion, a cobbler named William King, wore a crimson cape with the words "For God, the King, and the Commonwealth" embroidered upon it.[40]

Item: In a 1550 sermon, John Hooper (1495?-1555), declared that what compelled him to speak the truth was the "love I bear the King's majesty and to this commonwealth."[41]

Item: The radical Protestant John Ponet (1516?-1556) wrote in *A Short Treatise of Politike Power:* "Men ought to have more respect to their country than to their princes; to the commonwealth than to any one person. For the country and commonwealth is a degree above the king. Next to God men ought to love their country and the whole commonwealth before any member of it."[42]

Item: In a collection of verses for Elizabeth is found a song duet, dated 1559, between the Queen and England. "Who calls?" asks the Queen and "England" answers: "I am thy lover fair, / Has chosen thee to mine heir, / And my name is merry England." To this the Queen replied: "Here is my hand, my dear lover England, / I am thine both with mind and heart...." Shortly before the Armada encounter, the Queen visited her ships, and another song welcomed her thus:

> And many a captain kissed her hand,
> As she passed forth through every band,
> Where many a one did say and swear
> To live and die for England
> And would not ask a penny pay.....
> But of their own would find a stay
> To serve her Grace for England.[43]

Item: An author who flourished between 1587 and 1589, in

1585 penned a diatribe against English imitators of foreign manners that was entitled *The English Ape*. William Rankins, fearing that the infection might be England's undoing, forwarns his country in these words: "How hateful will it seem... when the bowels of that place which brought us forth, our country that nourrished us (for which every member is born to die)... be so altered... with the spotted imitation."[44]

Item: In *A Quip for an Upstart*, 1592, the pamphleteer and dramatist Robert Greene (1560?-1592), again rode the popular war horse, xenophobia, and expressed his fear for England's moral future. Then, he flung this at the Italians in England: "You come not alone but accompanied with a multitude of abominable vices,... wherewith you have infected this glorious Island... Get thee home again... and let me... live... in my native home in England, where I was born and bred."[45]

In the literary domain, there are, first of all, the translators who expressed their patriotic sentiments in the introductions to epistles. No longer would England trail behind the rest of Europe, either culturally or intellectually. In the mid-1550s, Henry Parker, Lord Morley (1476-1556), revealed in the dedicatory letter of his translation of Petrarch's *Trionfi* with how much bitterness he had not long ago watched a French translator dedicate to the French king his version of these poems. Then and there, Morley had decided to do the same and present his translation to the English king.[46] Th. Hoby (1530-1566) also remarked on the advantage other countries possessed when it came to translations. He regretted England's laggardliness in bringing a book as admirable as this *Courtier*, which he had translated, to everybody's attention, when it had been known in all other languages long before. Translations increased erudition; England should do more in that field, "that we alone of the world may not be still counted barbarous in our tongue.... And so shall perchance in time become as famous in England as the learned men of other nations.[47]

In 1581, George Pettie (1548-1589) complained in an Epistle to the Reader introducing his translation, *Civile*

Conversation of M. Steeven Guazzo, that Englishmen behave badly and vilify their own country. They imitate what they hear foreigners say about England and thereby reinforce unjust opinions. But, he exclaimed, "I am persuaded that those which know it, and love it, will report it for the civilest country in the world: and if it be thought to be otherwise by strangers, the disorders of those travellers abroad are the chief cause of it."[48] Pettie had more to say on England's virtues but his main concern was the defense of the mother tongue.

On this question, minds were divided also as to what profited national honor more: would English culture be better served by a classically educated elite who communicated their thoughts in Latin, or should native authors demonstrate the efficacy of their own language? The defenders of the vernacular were themselves divided between extremists, who wanted to keep English free of foreign admixture, of "inkhorn" words, and those who maintained that a language must steadily enrich itself with imports and neologisms. George Pettie continued his Epistle by denouncing those who disdained English, those with "such queasy stomachs that nothing will down with them than French, Italian, or Spanish," those who admired even poorly written foreign books, which were clearly improved by an English translation. These fools could not detect mistakes in foreign works and therefore admired them, while they were totally ignorant of the advantages of the mother tongue which one understood fast and retained better.

Yet worst of all was that people claimed that English could not express as much as did other languages because English was still barbaric.[49] One wonders whether anyone in 1581 still held such views. The argument must have been tired and old-hat by then. As early as 1553, Thomas Wilson (1525?-1581) had, in his *Arte of Rhetorique,* recommended the use of natural English, without "inkhorn" terms. He had scolded those who "seek so far outlandish English that they forget altogether their mother's tongue." When they come home from travels abroad, "they will powder their talk with oversea language. He that comes lately out of France, will talk

French English... Another chops in with Angleso Italiano."
He also had harsh words for Latinists who "will so Latine their
tongue that the simple cannot but wonder at their talk."[50]

In the latter part of the century, English literature as
well as the language stimulated only praises for their
accomplishments.[51] And even inveterate Latinists like Ascham
(1515-1568) finally began to write in their own language,
although persisting in apologizing for it.[52] Foxe had first
written his martyrology in Latin, then remade it into an
English document. But when he sent a copy to his alma mater
in Oxford, he found it appropriate to derogate English, saying:
"To me it seems scarcely fit for your library, especially as it is
written in English and not in Latin... I am only grieved that the
book is not written in Latin, and so more pleasant to your
reading, but the needs of the common people of our land drove
me to the vernacular."[53] At last, however, a cultured
schoolman, who had a profound sense for language, explained
at length why Englishmen should learn English, and study it
with the same earnest application and solicitude the ancient
languages had attracted. It was Richard Mulcaster's (1530?-
1611) remarkable discourse that culminated in the well-known
sentence: "I love Rome, but London better, I favor Italy, but
England more, I honor the Latin, but I worship the English."[54]
What the mother tongue meant for sixteenth-century Englishmen cannot be better attested to than by another speech from
the same Shakespeare play that introduced this chapter. Exiled
Mowbray laments:

> The language I have learn't these forty years,
> My native English now I must forgo;
> And now my tongue's use is to me no more
> Than an unstringed viol or a harp....
> Within my mouth you have engaol'd my tongue....
> What is thy sentence [then] but speechless death,
> Which robs my tongue from breathing native breath!
>
> *Richard II,* act 1, scene 3

The End of the Triumphal Entry, woodcut
by Donat Hubschmann, c. 1563

Conclusion

The abundance of examples should leave little doubt as to the existence of nationalism in the sixteenth century, and of a nationalism that differed in no essential way from any later kind. It was then, as it was to be in the nineteenth century, a well-articulated emotion, shared by all professions and classes that have left us their opinions. Often vocal to the point of shrillness and foolishness, it was not, as has been alleged, the property of an elite or limited to love for one's home region or for the ruling dynasty. If we ask about nationalism's place in the scale of contemporary preoccupations, in comparison to art, humanism, and, especially, to religion, we must plead ignorance. The three latter subjects have been worked over so intensively that our understanding for other notions might be clouded. For, what has been more often treated appears to have been more prevalent in reality. While the sixteenth century was eminently religion oriented, indeed, we cannot overlook the fact that religion was intimately entangled with politics, with economics, and, for that matter, with astrology. A whole chapter could be filled with contemporary voices accusing individuals or groups of using religion as a pretext for all sorts of evil intentions. We have only touched upon this sort of accusation. We cannot overlook that every denomination was eventually, if not from its very beginning, appropriated by political powers. Indeed, only those cults that were supported by the political arm could survive and become recognized religions.

    Nationalism rests quite comfortably next to, behind, or under most emotions that are for a while burning issues in a given society. We have an exemplary demonstration of it in our days, where clamor for a socialist life-style and economy—an international ideology—coexists with resolutely self-centered expressions of hatred against all foreignness considered harmful to the country's true national (or racial) past and destiny.

Which of the two concepts is the more compelling, the more far reaching? And which will appear the more significant to historians 400 years from now?

NOTES

INTRODUCTION

1. "It is our misfortune," complains R. Mousnier (1966, p. 67), "that all important words have more than one meaning. Would that they had one only and that one well fixed."
2. Among the many doubts expressed about the reliability of history, these three appear particularly appropriate: "All views of historical change are conditioned by how events have been recorded, stored, retrieved, and transmitted," Eisenstein 1966, p. 61. "What survives, survives largely by chance," C. S. Lewis, introduction to *The Oxford History of English Literature*. "We have only recorded opinion to go on. Of all the opinions... only a small fraction are now available... We have no way of knowing how widespread any opinion may have been in a semi-literate society," Boas 1969, p. 60.
3. The word is placed between quotation marks because its meaning has by now become all too dubious; we rarely meet it today without apologies and qualifications. Its greatest drawback, it seems to me, is its tradition-charged, intoxicating effect, and the difficulty of escaping its fairyland aura. Arguments for cautious use of the term can be found, again, in C. S. Lewis' *The Oxford History of English Literature*, pp. 55-65; and in Bush 1956, pp. 15 ff; Butterfield 1959, p. 343; Packard 1964, pp. 3-12; and Brown 1960, pp. 29-30, 38-42.
4. It would follow, then, that antiquity knew and expressed the idea.
5. "National sentiment is generally indistinguishable from... patriotism," reflects Johannet (1923, p. 16). Rivoire (1950, p. 7) says that the eighteenth century bandied the expression about without rhyme or reason, and with no one sure what was meant; he even adds that it is undefinable. Lately, Godechot (1971) has undertaken to define and distinguish the words "nation," "nationalism," and "patriotism" for the eighteenth century and for the French Revolution.
6. Kirn 1943, p. 79, and, similarly, pp. 35, 92.
7. Hertz [1951], p. 412.
8. Meinecke 1927, pp. 13-14.
9. Gaetano 1967, p. 138; La Noue 1967, pp. xviii, xxvii (introduction by F. E. Sutcliffe); Chabod 1967, pp. 593.
10. Chabod 1967, "Esiste uno stato del Rinascimento?" pp. 593-604.
11. Boas 1969, pp. 218-219.
12. Hobsbawm 1967, p. 132; Mombauer 1936, pp. 75-76.

89

13. Lefebvre (1935, pp. 250-61) is of the opinion that the term is an anachronism until the time of the Dreyfuss affair; Soboul (1960) doesn't mention nationalism at all, nor does Godechot (1965). In his earlier work (1963), Godechot had agreed with Lefebvre's opinion of the term's anachronism for the revolutionary period, but he concedes that the revolution had incited national feelings in France. He refuses, however, to allow nationalism any existence in the first years of the revolution, an opinion pursued in his article mentioned above, note 5 (1971). Rudé (1971, p. 3) flatly states that historians agree that the revolution was the product of social conflicts. At the end of the nineteenth century, Lord Acton (1907, pp. 276, 281) had gone so far as to deny expressly that the revolution had launched any national sentiments.

14. Hobsbawm 1967, p. 137. According to this author, there were in all of Europe and during the whole nineteenth century only two genuinely popular liberation movements: the Irish Repeal Act of 1839 and the Greek wars of independence of 1821-1829 (see pp. 138, 140ff).

15. Kaiser 1961, ch. 12; Körig 1937, pp. 22 ff; Hertz 1957, pp. 457-58; Meinecke 1959, pp. 430 ff, for Herder's uneasiness in the matter, and pp. 485 ff, for Goethe's feelings; Cassirer 1955, pp. 230-33.

16. Treitschke 1886, vol. 2, p. 96.

17. Eyck 1955.

18. "The common people in each region, and even the intellectual elite, spoke their mutually unintelligible dialects and lacked the least vestiges of national consciousness." So judges D. M. Smith in the "Risorgimento" section of *The Modern Cambridge History*, vol. 10, ch. 21. In the same vein, see Hobsbawm 1967, pp. 136-37, and Molfese 1964, pp. 12-15.

19. L. Chevalier (1958) indicates clearly what preoccupied the lower classes in the first half of the nineteenth century. He also, and rather incidently, reveals the survival of regional traits and regional hostility in long-unified France (pp. 364 ff).

20. A historian of natural sciences, praising the wonders of scientific thinking that arose in the seventeenth century, says: "It is doubtful whether anything else so original as this ever happened in all the rest of European history, *unless it is perhaps the comparable development of historical science and historical consciousness in the nineteenth century*" (my emphasis). Butterfield 1959, pp. 34-35.

21. The assumption of a common name is the first move toward conscious national individualization for Kisch (1943, p. 57).

22. Lemberg 1964, vol. 1, pp. 103, 148 ff; vol. 2, p. 71.

PORTUGAL

1. Bourdon (1970, pp. 7-8) stresses Portugal's precocity and obstinacy as her national characteristic.

2. Quieroz Veloso in Peres and Cerdeira 1927-38, vol. 5, p. 24; Livermore 1947, p. 251.

3. Queiroz Veloso 1927-38, pp. 36-37; Livermore 1947, p. 252.

4. Rebello da Silva 1864, pp. 1-11.

5. Ibid., the whole first volume.

6. Ibid., p. 519; Queiroz Veloso 1927-38, p. 200; Almeida 1922-29, vol. 2, p. 458; Livermore 1947, p. 265.

7. Rebello da Silva 1864, pp. 517, 522; Almeida 1922-29, pp. 455-58; Queiroz Veloso 1927-38, pp. 197 ff.
8. Livermore 1947, pp. 270 ff; Bourdon 1970, pp. 46 ff; Martins 1894, vol. 2, pp. 70-80.
9. Storck 1897, p. 728; Jayne 1910, p. 277; Schneider 1930, pp. 235-36; Le Gentil 1954, p. 26.
10. Le Gentil 1954, p. 196.
11. Bataillon 1952, p. 170; Bierlaire 1968, p. 96; Feist Hirsch 1967, p. 24; Bell 1941, p. 245. It is, however, possible that Damião did not have to learn Latin as such but only versification abroad: see Vocht 1934, p. 613.
12. Bataillon 1952, pp. 175-77; Silva Rego 1959, p. 14.
13. Beau (1937) treats precisely this fusion of linguistics with nationalism.
14. Ibid., pp. 73-75, 80.
15. Ibid., pp. 76-77.
16. Ibid., pp. 77-80. The argument of language as a weapon was most likely taken over from Nebrija. See pp. 25 and 92, notes 27-30.
17. Ibid., p. 82.
18. See *Paladinos de Linguagem* (1922-26), edited by Agostinho da Campos; three volumes, with texts relating to the sixteenth century in vol. 1, pp. 4-87.

SPAIN

1. Pulgar 1943, vol. 1, pp. 452 ff, relating events of the year 1482.
2. Arco 1939, pp. 315 ff, with texts of royal instructions for dealing with papal delegates in Spain.
3. *Il Principe*, ch. 21. "Do we know," observes Mattingly (1964, p. 143), "how much his [Ferdinand's] pious phrases were meant to deceive others, and how much to appease the uneasiness of his spirit?"
4. Alfonso de Valdés, *Diálogo de Lactancio y un arcediano* (1527). Marcel Bataillon (1924, p. 34), who, it is safe to say, knows everything about Erasmus and Spain, doubts that Erasmus "would have insinuated, as did A. de Valdés, that the military outrage was a divine punishment." He notes the same mixture of Erasmian peacefulness and Spanish imperialism in J. L. Vives in "Du nouveau sur Vives" (1930). In his *Erasme et l'Espagne* (1937, p. 434), Batallon again stresses the pronounced nationalism in the Spanish Easmians; on pp. 415-16, he speaks of Valdés's defense of the sack of Rome.
5. Lynch 1961, p. 23. For the growing bitterness between Spain and Rome, see Philippson 1878 and Pavolini 1941.
6. Sandoval 1955-56, vol. 1, p. 128.
7. Ibid., pp. 128, 199, 216. Identical demands were made in other cities during the uprisings of the years 1520-21: see Seaver 1928, pp. 137, 166, 175, 277.
8. Looz-Corswarem 1931, pp. 32, 52.
9. Mariana 1839-40, "Prólogo del autor."
10. Mesnard (1969, p. 566), speaking of Mariana's complex personality, says that his ecclesiastical mentality was deformed by national pride. Cirot 1905, pp. 135, 333; Lewy 1960, pp. 79, 102, 162-63; Salcedo y Ruiz 1928, p. 465.
11. Astraín 1912-20, vol. 3, pp. 99-100.
12. Ibid., p. 100.
13. Ibid., pp. 99, 100.
14. Ibid., p. 102. Jesuits in other countries seem not to have favored foreign

officers either. See Boehmer 1928, p. 92; Sicroff 1960, p. 280; Fouqueray 1910-25, vol. 1, p. 487.
15. Sicroff 1960, pp. 182 ff.
16. Astraín 1912-20, vol. 3, p. 589..
17. Ibid., p. 590.
18. Lewy 1960, p. 124. This author sees Mariana as even more of a nationalist than had Cirot, fifty years earlier. Lewy thinks that the Spanish clergy in general was both royalist and nationalistic. For Mariana's stand against blood purity, see Lewy 1960, p. 103.
19. Sicroff 1960, pp. 290 ff; Bataillon 1925, pp. 14-15.
20. Sicroff 1960, p. 294.
21. We read, for example, in the chronicler Florian de Ocampo (1791-92, vol. 1, p. 47) that Tubal was Noah's grandson and came to Spain 144 years after the Flood. Cf. Sicroff 1960, p. 294; Cirot 1905, p. 285; Koenigsberger 1975, pp. 155 ff, about the Spanish historians and their origin myths.
22. Sicroff 1960, p. 294.
23. Boehmer 1928, p. 92.
24. Kamen 1965, pp. 49-66, 304.
25. Bataillon 1937, p. 530.
26. Pastor 1929; Romera-Navarro 1929.
27. "The most grandiose prologue ever to have been placed at the head of a grammer," H. Meier calls it (1935, p. 15).
28. Weisgerber [1948], "Die Sprache als compañera del imperio," pp. 76-81.
29. Nebrija 1946, p. 5 (prologue).
30. About the often repeated, and apparently always ineffective, orders to speak only Latin at the University of Salamanca, see Olmedo 1944, pp. 157 ff; Ocete 1946, pp. 162 ff. For the struggle between Latin and Spanish, see Romera-Navarro 1929. The editors of Nebrija's Grammar (see Nebrija 1946, p. xxix) say that Nebrija's true vocation was the rejuvenation of Latin in Spain. The rector of the University of Salamanca, Perez de Oliva, was praised by his nephew Morales in a Discorso for his love of the native tongue, while his Latin was so excellent that, had he cared to use it, he could have made a more distinguished name for himself. Luíz de Granada (Luíz de León) was called the most famous Latin orator. For his Latin style, see Switzer 1927. On the other hand, Ticknor (1965, vol. 2, p. 100 n.) shows Luíz's fervent interest in Spanish. Analysis of Luíz's linguistic ideas were found in Guy 1943.
31. Rosales and Vivanco 1940.
32. Ibid., vol. 1, pp. 567-71; Entwistle 1947.
33. Cervantes, Obras completas (1917-23), vol. 7, pp. 11-111; Vicente 1950, vol. 1, pp. 239-56.
34. Ibid., vol. 7, pp. 219-26. Castro, in his (French-language) Cervantès (1931, p. 17), writes: "At the time of writing the Algiers pieces, Spain's cause was...that of Cervantes," and the letter to the royal secretary "was a simple echo of the imperialistic idea that Cervantes shared with the least of his countrymen."
35. And yet, Luíz de León, the mystic, found in the Bible prophecies for Spaniards, the predestined people: see Bell 1925, pp. 280-81.
36. Ticknor 1965, vol. 2, ch. 27; Pfandl 1929, ch. 4.
37. M. Chevalier 1966, p. 123.
38. Ibid. One could mention in this connection the chauvinistic Bishop Vincentius Hispanus, who in the thirteenth century, reminded Frenchmen and Germans that Charlemagne and his twelve peers had been defeated by Spaniards: see Post 1953 and 1954.
39. Ticknor 1965, vol. 2, p. 595. On nationalistic excesses, see Pfandl 1929, pp. 129-32, 151 ff.

40. How deeply embedded in the past lay the "vision of Spain as a splendid Platonic idea," and how acceptable even to modern Spaniards is the "Platonic" idea of *hispanidad*, has been treated recently by Koenigsberger (1975, p. 144).

ITALY

1. Guicciardini 1953: Considerazioni, ch. 12. A century earlier, Leonardo Bruni had, in his republican fervor, blamed imperial Rome for having crushed flourishing Italian cities. See Baron 1968, vol. 1, p. 165. Toward the end of the sixteenth century, Guicciardini's observation was revived and amplified by Scipio Ammirato, who demonstrated that unification would have been a disaster for Italy, as it would have been for ancient Greece: *Discorsi sopra C. Tacitus* 5. 53–62.

2. Burdach and Piur 1913-28, vol. 2, p. 337, for the indestructible pretensions of the modern Romans; G. Voigt 1880, vol. 2, p. 365; Curcio 1928, pp. 179-224. In the twelfth century, Otto von Freising had described a meeting between his nephew, Emperor Frederich I, and a Roman delegation full of "Roman" delusions, detailing the emperor's cool reminder of the true situation: *Gesta Frederici* 2. 31-33.

3. Lorenzo Valla 1544, preface to *De linguae latinae elegantia*.

4. Baron 1955, vol. 1, pp. 49-52, and 1968, pp. 243 ff; Dante, *Il Convito* 1. 3.

5. *Storia di Milano*, vol. 7, pp. 285, 287.

6. Paruta 1943, vol. 2, p. 147.

7. Annio di Viterbo, as cited in Asher 1969, p. 413.

8. The cities kept in military training by constantly warring among themselves. For Italy's gifted military theorists, see F. L. Taylor 1921; Pieri 1952, pp. 612-13; J. R. Hale 1965.

9. Gilbert 1954 and 1965. Both studies give numerous examples of nationally concerned authors, although Gilbert, like Chabot (1967, pp. 593 ff), is not convinced of an authentic sense of nationalism in Italy at that time. Rather, he stresses the overwhelming local selfishness of the cities and sees in expressions of nationalism nothing but humanistic rhetoric, or political "good form." The same argument is taken up by Major (1969, pp. 30-31). There can be no quarrel about political incompetence in the matter of Italian unification, but what is of interest here is the eternal national nostalgia. Whether political opportunism or humanistic rhetoric, it still was national consciousness.

10. See titles such as Alberti's *Descrizione di tutta Italia* (1553); Giannotti's *Discorso delle cose d'Italia* (1819, vol. 3); Vettori's *Sommario della storia d'Italia* (1848); and Guicciardini's *Storia d'Italia* (1953).

11. Gilbert (1954, p. 41) writes that for the fifteenth-century humanists it was a point of honor to praise their hometowns without losing sight of the greater unit, and (p. 42) that with the first French invasion (1494), "a feeling of the common fate of the Italians had entered the political consciousness." Yes, indeed. It would seem to be in contradiction to the author's opinion elsewhere (see note 9, above) and more in keeping with what Kirn (1943, p. 13) found: that today, as in the past, national loyalty is quite compatible with love for one's native city. Monod (1895-97, p. 16) noticed the very same cohabitation of loyalties as far back as the ninth century.

12. If we lump admirers of Italy together under the name of humanists, we may

roughly differentiate Italian-haters as antipapists, anti-Machiavellians, and all those who resented Italian competion in their professions.

13. *Arte della guerra*, bk. 7, ch. 24.
14. *Lettere*, 10 August 1513.
15. *Lettere*, 26 August 1513.
16. Cf. Gilbert 1954 and 1965, as cited in note 9.
17. *Lettere*, 17 May 1526.
18. Ridolfi 1967, p. 255.
19. Guicciardini 1953, "Appendi" to the *Ricordi*, no. 9.
20. Even Chabod (1967, p. 596) concedes that after 1535 Guicciardini had more sober thoughts on Italian conditions, that something seemed to be stirring in the country, that now Venice—long accused of being the archenemy of Italy's freedom—was considered a defender of Italy's good name.
21. The calling upon foreign troops cannot be said to be particular to Italy or to the sixteenth century. Defensive and offensive treaties have always been, and are still today, arranged with outside powers, as soon as the situation seems to require it.
22. "Seldom... has a generation been so satisfied with itself and with the world around it," remarks Cochrane (1965, p. 13).
23. Tocco 1924 and 1926; Curcio 1934, ch. 7, "Il Patriotismo"; Cian 1936.
24. How little justified Italy was in calling all foreigners barbarians has been well demonstrated in Hay 1960.
25. Chronologically, Boiardo does not fit into the self-imposed limits of the years 1500-1600. Yet, thematically, he does belong here. To interrupt one's poetic work out of patriotic sorrow is surely unusual, if that was his authentic reason. Fourteen ninety-four when Boiardo broke off his writing, was the year of the first French invasion, a date that many Italians considered to be the fateful moment of the national downfall.
26. Cicero had given them the idea that some divine benevolence had created the Alps in order to shield Italians from barbarians (in *De Provinciis*).
27. Curcio 1934, p. 185 n; Tocco 1926, pp. 5-7; Cian 1936, pp. 160-73; Mango 1886, especially pp. 22 ff, 172-73.
28. Olschki (1922, ch. 3, "Struggle against Latin") shows how the subterranean current of vernacular usage emerged and was energetically furthered by an impressive number of learned, articulate, and very impatient Italians; also Buck 1952, especially pp. 98-135; H. W. Klein 1967.
29. Bloch (1949, p. 126) reflects on the mental difficulty, even disturbance. created by communicating native thoughts in a foreign idiom. Baruzi (1922, p. 40) draws attention, more specifically, to the mystic's need to express his innermost experiences in the vulgar tongue, and not in Latin. Olschki (1922, p. 170) summarizes the Italians' worry over, and anger at, the danger of habits molded by ancient thought patterns, habits that no power on earth might ever be able to break.
30. See Vernon Hall 1945, pp. 25-36; Grayson 1960, pp. 414, 421-28, 431-32; Kristeller 1965, ch. 7, "Origin... of the... Italian Prose," pp. 119-41, as well as the rich bibliography.
31. Sigonio 1737, vol. 7, cols. 521-28; Cian 1911, p. 295.
32. Giovio 1577, p. 222.
33. Doni 1928, vol. 1, p. 191.
34. Stella 1965, pp. 160, 161.
35. Tocco 1926, p. 330.
36. Passerin 1947, p. 8.

GERMANY

To circumvent the confusion as to what constituted the *Reich*, the search for national concern has been limited to the land known as Germany for the last 100 years or so extending to the end of the Second World War, including, however, the Netherlands and Austria as birthplaces or residences of emperors.

1. Schulte 1933, pp. 29, 33, 35—36; Gerlich 1960, pp. 368; 370; Rörig 1937, p. 9; Lintzel 1961, pp. 208 ff.
2. Rörig 1937, p. 10, and 1948; Schulte 1933, p. 23; Conrad 1962, vol. 1, p. 222.
3. The subject of Germany's ancient and never-compromised liberty was stressed again and again in political journalism, in the humanists' history writings, in proclamations of the estates, and for their own good reasons, by French declarations of support of anti-Habsburg parties in Germany. See Waldeck 1910, p. 11; Schottenloher 1922, p. 200. Germany's break with Rome might not have been so radical were it not for the centuries-old demands of liberation from papal interference in German affairs and from its financial obligations to Rome. While mainly for the same reasons, the break in other countries was effected by the heads of government, in Germany it was initiated by lower strata of the society.
4. F. H. Schubert 1966. This important study stresses the checks and balances in government. The author also emphasizes the interest in German affairs shown by foreign political thinkers, who in their own countries felt uneasy about the trend toward absolutism. See index of Schubert, references to Bodin, Hooker, and the "Monarchomachen"; also the same author's essay, "Französische Staatstheorie" (1968, pp. 31 ff, 55 ff). For Germany's constant fear of imperial domination, see Hartung 1950, p. 326; Schröcker 1950, p. 191; Dollmann 1927, p. 13; Fichtenau 1959, p. 16.
5. World-embracing aspirations were certainly no longer the concerns of Germany's actual rulers: the territorial princes, the estates, the electors. But the emperors still believed in, or held onto, the task of keeping the world together under one sceptre and one faith, which was also the daily bread of the German humanists, partly by conviction, partly for rhetorical reasons.
6. Offler (1965, p. 226) called it a mixture of the "parochially narrow with the ecumenically wide."
7. Liebmann 1910, p. 16; Aubin 1938, p. 143; Hartung 1950, p. 16; Schulte 1933, p. 121; and G. Strauss 1959, pp. 40 ff, about the cartographers' despair. However, with due respect for differences of degree, the problems of fixed borders and unified administration were far from solved in France, as can be seen in Doucet 1948, vol. 1, pp. 15–39.
8. Hartung 1911, p. 322.
9. On the importance of a *Hausmacht*, see Bader 1954, p. 79; Ritter 1950, p. 64; Angermeier 1956, p. 196; Lutz 1964, pp. 11-12; Lhotsky 1971, p. 28.
10. Tiedemann [1913], p. 134; Diehl 1937, pp. 470 ff; Ritter 1950, p. 64. In fact, although electors had to be Germans, emperors were not by law confined to the nationality: Conrad 1962, vol. 1, p. 220.

11. Du Mont 1726-31, vol. 5, p. 298, para. ix; Zeumer 1913, vol. 2, pp. 309-13; Conrad 1962, vol. 2, p. 5; Kleinheyer 1968, pp. 23, 33, 43 ff, 49, 65.

12. The imperial title and status had tempted English and French courts for centuries, if sporadically. When Maximmillian I's reign came to an end, it looked as if the emperorship was no longer a strictly German affair. England and, infinitely more vigorously, France now showed intense interest in the imperial succession. For the disturbance that this situation aroused in French minds, see, for instance, Budé's letters to Erasmus of 15 February and 6 March 1519(Op. Ep., vol. 3, pp. 480, 503). For the wheeling and dealing prior to the election, see Spalatin 1851, pp. 40 ff, 108; the letter from Jacob Fugger to Charles V (1523) forcefully reminding the emperor of the Fuggers' role in gaining the crown for him, in Jansen 1910, pp. 249-50; Pölnitz 1949, vol. 1, p. 518; and Pauli 1862, with diplomatic sources. For the long history of French interest in the imperial crown, see Kern 1910, especially ch. 12; Zeller 1934; and Francois, 1958.

13. This double-headed opposition led in 1530 to the formation of an anti-Habsburg League, the *Schmalkaldische Bund*, by Protestant German princes with cordial support from foreign monarchs. Besides this sufficiently dangerous association, there were other local nobles who, condottieri-like, made antiimperial politics on their own. Charles defeated the *Bund* in 1547. It turned out to be the beginning of his own eventual checkmate: Fabian 1962.

14. Maximilian I (1459-1519) was born and died in Austria; Charles V (1500-1558), born in the Netherlands, died in Spain; Ferdinand I (1503-1564), born in Spain, died in Austria; Maximilian II (1527-1575), born in Austria, died in Germany; Rudolf II (1552-1612), born in Austria, died in Bohemia.

15. Elections took place in Frankfurt, coronations in Aachen (later in Frankfurt too). The High Tribunal sat in Speyer, while the Imperial Diets met in a number of "imperial" cities. Money for elections and the many other needs of emperors came mainly from Augsburg. On questions of imperial residences, see Schulte 1936; Heimpel 1941; and Berges 1952. An eighteenth-century historian, Moser (1767, p. 417), writes that electors made attempts to draw emperors closer to the places of political action.

16. One author has spoken of a "Turkish-Crusade complex" in Maximilian (cited by Wagner 1969, p. 43), but, actually, the Turkish-Crusade complex seemed quite widespread in sixteenth-century Europe, and in respect to Maximilian it must be remembered how dangeroulsy close the Austrian lands of Habsburg were to the advancing Turks.

17. For Maximilian, see Waas 1966, p. 187; Wiesflecker 1971, pp. 414-15. For Charles, see Rassow 1932; Brandi 1937, pp. 307 ff; Lutz 1964, pp. 23 ff; Rabe 1971, p. 456.

18. For widely differing opinions on Maximilian: Lhotsky 1971, p. 456; Wiesflecker 1971, pp. 11-43.

19. See p. 22 for the Spanish insistence on having and retaining a genuinely Spanish king.

20. Requests similar to those made by the Spanish estates were written by the German electors into the conditions to which the imperial candidates were to swear, and especially into those presented to Charles: he was not to name foreigners to imperial posts, nor to bring foreign troops into the country without the Diet's consent; the official language was to be German, unless it were Latin. Du Mont 1726-31, vol. 4, p. 289, paras. 13-14; Hartung 1911, p. 382.

21. Hartung 1910, pp. 5 ff; Fischer-Galati 1959, p. 114; Lutz 1964, pp. 82-83; Lhotsky 1971, p. 78.

22. Foreigners were generally favorably impressed by Germany. What they invariably admired were the orderly, well-provisioned cities, the wealth of the population, the excellence of the artisans, and the inventions, printing, of course, above all.

23. When, in contrast, the Duke of Anjou, who had with great difficulty been made king of Poland, succeeded his brother on the French throne, he immediately abandoned Poland to the dismay of his Polish subjects. Apparently, it occurred to no one that he could rule either country from afar. We may, however, consider the reverse possibility, the case in which a prince would have been called away from France to his duty in Poland: he might not have been in the same hurry. Similarly, Germany suffered neglect because the country was, or seemed, less attractive to Charles than Spain, Italy, or his homeland, the Netherlands.

24. Hartung 1910, p. 169, 1911, p. 344, and 1950, pp. 34-35. Also Lutz 1964, pp. 485-86; Schubert 1968, p. 20.

25. Schubert 1966, for the importance of the Diets, and 1968, p. 20, for the traditional institutions, in general.

26. Herding 1965, p. 141.

27. J. Wagner 1929, pp. 56 ff; Ritter 1950, p. 64; Schubert 1966, pp. 98-111, 172-73, 179, 184, 204, 230; Wiesflecker 1971, pp. 11-12.

28. Quoted in Offler 1956, p. 220.

29. Misch 1930; Lhotsky 1944 and 1963; Coreth 1950; Schröcker 1950, p. 193; Lutz 1964, p. 486; Waas 1966, p. 187; Schubert 1966, pp. 190-212, "Aetas Maximilianea"; Wagner 1969; and Wiesflecker 1971, p. 414. In all these studies the role of the German humanists is underlined.

30. On Piccolomini's place in the history of German humanism: Joachimsen 1910, pp. 27, 32, 46, and 1971, pp. 282-84; Tiedemann [1913], pp. vii, viii, 6-7, 14, 24 ff, 35, 84 n., 116, 137; Paul 1936, pp. 25-26 (on p. 57, Paul has listed the themes that the humanists adapted from Aeneas' various writings); Langosch's 1962 edition of Piccolomini's *Germania* (p. 13). For Piccolomini's influence on German cosmographers, see G. Strauss 1959, pp. 14 ff.

31. Two things, however, had certainly changed in the three centuries: the vernaculars had won out over Latin, and scientific progress and scientific seriousness had done away with fantasies of national or racial origins, which, in the sixteenth century, had run the gamut from the Trojans and Druids to diverse sons of Noah, unless they were autochthonous.

32. In *Germania ad rem publicam Argentinensem* (1501). In 1505, Wimpfeling published his *Epitoma Germanorum*, regarded as the first tentative history of Germany.

33. *Urbis Norimbergae ... de origine, situ, moribus et institutis descriptio* (1502).

34. Joachimsen 1910, ch. 6, pp. 155-95, on *Germania illustrata*.

35. *Epitome laudum Sueuorum.*

36. Titles of Bebel's writings are in *Opera Bebeliana*; some of the works are reprinted in the seventeenth-century collection of Schardius, *Germanicarum rerum* (1673, vol. 1, pp. 95 ff).

37. D. F. Strauss 1914; Joachimsen 1910, p. 183; Tiedemann [1913], pp. xxi, 83; Schubert 1966, particularly pp. 195-96, 203-207.

38. Hutten 1859-69, vol. 3, pp. 353-400.

39. Ibid., vol. 5, pp. 101-134, "Ad principes germanos...."

40. See above note 12.

41. Goez 1958; Ullmann 1949.
42. That the same claims were made by other Europen countries, local colors aside, cannot be stressed too often.
43. Gattinara, Charles V's chancellor, begins his advice to the young emperor with these words: "Sire, since God the creator gave you the grace of raising you in dignity above all kings and princes of Christendom, making you the greatest emperor and king since the distribution of power made in the person of Charlemagne, your predecessor...." Cited in Bornate [1915], p. 405.
44. To the titles in notes 17, 18, and 29, there should be added here Fichtenau 1965. The author maintains, convincingly, that Maximilian was most probably equally attracted by the ideas of universality and of nationalism.
45. Janssen 1863-72, vol. 2, pp. 739-41.
46. Ibid., pp. 772-24, 799-802, 956-59.
47. Spalatin 1851, pp. 140-44.
48. Ibid., p. 204.
49. Ibid., pp. 205-6.
50. Ibid., pp. 143-44, 219-20.
51. Ibid., pp. 219-20.
52. Ansheim, *Berner Chronik*, vols. 3-4, pp. 1-3.
53. Spalatin 1851, pp. 93, 96-97.
54. Hortleder 1618, vol. 2, pp. 214-15.
55. Druffel 1873-82, vol. 2, pp. 198-200.
56. Ibid., vol. 3, p. 512.
57. Ibid., pp. 533-34. "Beloved fatherland" is mentioned several times.
58. Ibid., pp. 553-57.
59. Hühns 1968, pp. 1040-41.
60. Druffel 1873-82, vol. 3, 384-93.
61. Chabod (1967, pp. 597-98) seems to think so.
62. Ascham 1904, pp. 153 ff, on Maurice, Elector of Saxony.
63. The captain's name was Vogelsberger. In Liliencron (1869, vol. 4, pp. 477-79), several songs bemoan the captain's fate and accuse instead the emperor and his commissary of treachery.
64. Ibid., pp. 584-85: a song that reproves and, at the same time, pities Metz, one of the cities that had not fought the transaction.
65. Treaty of Chambord, in Druffel 1873-82, vol. 3, pp. 340, 341.
66. Liliencron 1869: songs relating to our period are in vol. 4.
67. "Eines sechsischen meidlein klag und bitt." Ibid., pp. 460-62.
68. "Ein lied wider die feinde des evengelii, Mamelucken und vorrether ihres eigenen vaterlands." Ibid., pp. 462-63.
69. "Ein lied und vermanung an die Landsknechte, dass sie der armen Christenheit und ihrem lieben vaterland beistehen." Ibid., pp. 500-504.
70. "Warhafte und gegründte meldung...der...tückischen...anschleg...so wider die löblichen protestierenden stende...durch die grossen feind Gottes, den babst und seinen anhang...zu verderben des deutschen lands erdacht sein....Ibid., pp. 302-310.
71. "Ein warnung an alle und iede ware liebhaber des heiligen evangelions Christi und freiheit der löblichen deutschen nation von Gott verliehen." Ibid., pp. 320-24.
72. Ibid., pp. 340-42.
73. See the devastating opinion of a fellow Protestant, in the shoemaker-rhymer Hans Sachs' *Werke* (1966, vol. 1, pp. 55 ff, 66 ff; vol. 2, pp. 379 ff). We find the Markgrave mentioned in Bodin's *République*, vol. 3, ch. 4, as an example of

a cruel despoiler of the land and the poor. On the other hand, he found an admirer in Roger Ascham, the English Protestant humanist and visitor to Germany. See Ryan 1963, pp. 177 ff.

74. The text is given in many collections of documents: Léonard 1693, vol. 2, pp. 484-91; Du Mont 1726-31, vol. 4, pp. 31 ff; Druffel 1873-82, vol. 3, 340-47.

75. Moritz von Sachsen, *Politische Korrespondenz des Herzogs und Kurfürsten Moritz von Sachsen* (1900-1904).

76. Sleidan 1556, pp. 753-55.

77. A. de Thou 1625, vol. 10, p. 210; and 1742, vol. 2, pp. 79-80. The arguments here used are virtually the same as Albrecht's in the following manifest.

78. Sleidan 1556, 755-57; Voigt 1852, vol. 1, pp. 272-75.

79. He refers here to the oath the emperor had taken at the time of his election. Cf. above, note 20.

80. Sleidan 1556, p. 757. |

81. Albrecht mentions the French king, of course, as an added menace.

82. Sleidan 1879, pp. 7-8, 137-40.

83. Grisar 1927, p. 111.

84. Tiedemann [1913], ch. 8 "Deutsche Sprache," pp. 80-89; Strauss 1959, pp. 142, 145 ff. According to Febvre and Martin 1955, pp. 481-83, the ratio of Latin books to German was fluctuating at the time. But if it seems to be an accepted fact that altogether more Latin than vernacular was printed at the time, the *printed* production cannot reflect the total material *written* in the vernacular and printed only much later, such as protocols, manifests, pamphlets, sermons, letters to and from persons who did not understand Latin.

85. See above, p. 45. On Trithemius, Arnold 1971; on the "catalogue," p. 123.

86. Ibid., p. 132 n.

87. Ibid.

88. Krantz 1893, proem.

89. Halbauer 1929, p. 122.

90. Irenicus, *Germaniae exegeseos* (1518), pp. xl, cxliii. Actually, the Germans were neither more nor less despised by neighboring or competing countries than any other people. To the remarks in note 22, above, could be added the lofty eulogy by Henri Estienne in 1574 of the book fair at Frankfurt and of German culture, *Francofordiense Emporium,* and also the ranking of Germany directly after Italy as helper in the reawakening of arts and sciences by Frenchmen, as, for instance, in Estienne Dolet 1536-38, vol. 2, cols. 1156-57; or in Peletier du Mans 1607, proem to bk. 1, p. 7.

91. See above, p. 45.

92. Tiedemann [1913], p. 81.

93. Sudhoff 1936, p. 56.

94. Olschki 1919, ch. 4, for Italian academies.

95. Sebastian Franck. *Chronica* (1565), p. 11v; Wimpfeling, *Epitoma rerum germanicarum* (1505), fol. 1; Bebel, "Laudum Sueuorum," in Schardius, *Germanorum rerum* (1673), vol. 1, p. 137; Pirckheimer, "Historia belli Svitensis," in Freher, *Rerum Germanicarum scriptores* (1717), vol. 4, p. 53. And Luther also complained in "An die Ratherren," *Werke,* vol. 4, p. 53.

96. Tiedemann [1913], pp. 84-88; Arnold 1971, pp. 78-83; but much later as well: see Feugère's edition (1958) of H. Estienne's *Traité de la comformité du language françois avec le grec nouveau,* introduction, pp. 4-6.

97. See above, p. 44, and note 28.

FRANCE

1. Wiesflecker 1971, p. 14; Schröcker 1950, p. 188, n. 25; Lhotsky 1971, p. 40.
2. Druffel 1873-82, vol. 3, p. 387. Cf. above, pp. 47, 49-52.
3. *Discorsi*, "Ritratto delle cose di Francia." In Machiavelli 1961-68, vol. 2, p. 173.
4. Albèri 1839-63, vol. 1, pp. 184, 209, 232 ff; vol. 3, p. 410. Successive ambassadors between 1535 and 1563 were equally struck by French unity, love of king, and obedience, unless they had all succumbed to a cliché of the time. One of the ambassadors, Marino, cites an unnamed Frenchman, who had complained to him that the king of the Franks was better nowadays called king of slaves (vol. 1, p. 233).
5. Birch 1749, p. 436.
6. Castiglione, *Il Cortigiano* (1894 edition), vol. 1, ch. 42, p. 19. Here an Italian speaker asserts that the French are proud only about their use of arms. Budé, for one, protested vigorously against Frenchmen who held such an opinion about themselves: Delaruelle 1907a, pp. 161-66. Yet we find as late as 1580 a French historian, Du Tillet, assuring us that the French prefer arms to letters: dedicatory letter to the king in Du Tillet's *Recueil des rois de France* (1580).
7. Erasmus, *Opus Epistolarum* (1906-58 edition), vol. 7, p. 36. Budé's reply is in Delaruelle's summarizing work (1907, pp. 217-18), and in the French translation of the correspondence by La Garanderie (1967, pp. 254-55).
7a. Saulnier 1951.
8. Besides the disjointed, convoluted style of the period, bemoaned by modern readers, we find the frankly episodic composition of a Montaigne or a Pasquier. Montaigne says in one of his comments on his method of writing (1958, vol. 3, essay 9, p. 234) that his pen occasionally goes astray "by licence, not by mistake," and that he knows that his titles do not always embrace the subjects of his essays. Pasquier amiably criticizes the discrepancy between Montaigne's titles and contents, which he explains with this lovely image: "His book is not a flowerbed with orderly squares and borders, but something like a prairie, helter-skelter, artlessly diversified with many flowers" (Pasquier 1966, bk. 18 letter no. 1). Pasquier, consciously or unconsciously, uses almost the same words to describe his own motley method (*Recherches* bk. 6, p. 44, in Pasquier 1633). Budé was quite aware of his own unclassical style, as he and Erasmus discussed their respective preferences in writing: Erasmus, *Opus Epistolarum*, nos. 480, 493 (La Garanderie 1967, pp. 77-92). Budé mentions his writing fever, the wind-swollen sail of his mind, which he is often unable to take in soon enough. At the end of his *De Contemptu*, (1520), he remarks again on his uncontrollable frenzy while writing.
9. Lemberg (1967, vol. 2, pp. 72, 92) speaks about both the urge toward, and the fallacies of, characterizing peoples. In general, writings of foreign travelers are enlightening sources of erroneous, imaginary, contradictory, and partisan opinions on a given country, unless, that is, we consider so many judgments, in praise as well as in condemnation, of nationals on themselves.
10. Royalism (the "eighth sacrament," as Renan called it) and the related terms of monarchy, centralization and absolutism, have been abundantly discussed. Some of the more insightful studies are the following: Hitier 1903; W. Mommsen 1939; Doucet 1948; Hartung and Mousnier 1955; Schramm 1960; Lapeyre 1967; and Major 1969, which presents the latest of the author's investigations of the relationship between French institutions and kings.
11. Bloch, *Les Rois thaumaturges* (1924), whose subtitle, *Etudes sur le caractère surnaturel...particulièrement en France et en Angleterre*, suggests, as do

some of the studies mentioned in the foregoing note, that the exaltation of royalty was not an exclusively French phenomenon.

12. Barrès 1965-68, p. 293.
13. Hanotaux 1932-74, vol. 1, p. 539.
14. Good luck and talented writers: this was, according to Sallust (*De Catilinae Conjuratione* 1. 8), the winning combination to which Athens owed her prestige in the world. Her actual deeds he thought vastly overpraised. He made two more observations in the same short paragraph; in due course, these were taken up by one or the other humanist, namely, that some peoples compose elegant books while others do the hard but necessary work. The other point was that, in effect, glory and immortality did depend on good writers. Another reason for France's success in impressing herself on the consciousness of the world is that, according to Lapeyre (1967, pp. 8-13), France possessed the vastest archives of Europe. If so, it is understandable that where so much history was being stored, it was most easily accessible. What is available will be more often treated, and frequent treatment, in turn, attracts more attention and so gains in importance.
15. The imperial crown and the possessions that went with it were one aspect only (cf. above, note 12, to Germany). It was the prestige of the title that had led medieval French legists to create the formula that the French king is emperor in his realm: Hitier 1903, p. 75; Church 1931, p. 64; Doucet 1948, vol. 1, p. 75; Schramm 1960, p. 238; Wilks 1963, pp. 428-31; Lutz 1964, p. 8. The appellation "Holy King of the Franks" was, it seems, coined to counterbalance the "Holy Roman Emperor": see Wilks 1963, p. 430; Church 1931, p. 46. French authors often use the terms "empire" or "empire and kingdom" in connection with France: for instance, Du Tillet (1580) twice in his "Epître au Roy."

For later attempts to gain the imperial crown, see Zeller 1934, pp. 66-71, for Henry of Navarre's efforts. Also, Duplessis-Mornay 1824-25, vol. 2, pp. 213-17; Dotzauer 1966. Beyond any doubt, the most intriguing evidence for lingering French misgivings in the matter of the respective standings of kings and emperors are two pages of the Sun King's *Mémoires* from the year 1661 (see *Oeuvres de Louis XIV*, vol. 1, pp. 76-77, 1806 edition). He here assures his son of the exalted position of the French kings, which ought to have guaranteed precedence to their ambassadors in the company of those of the emperor. Due to papal intrigue, this was not the case, the king writes, except at the court of the Sultan. Zeller (1934, p. 523) comments on these remarks to the effect that evidently "Louis XIV's greatness did not prevent him from being bitten by the imperial itch." For us, the passage is the more astonishing because today only a specialist would know for sure who was the German emperor in 1661. (He was Leopold I.)
16. Kelley 1970; Bowen 1950; Cardascia 1943.
17. Barrillon 1897-99, vol. 1, 282-83; Doucet 1948, vol. 2, p. 868. This author calls foreign experts that "race eternally accursed as much as [they are] irreplacable." Picot 1888, vol. 2, p. 393.
18. Allut 1859, pp. 201-205; Simar 1911, p. 13; Mönch 1936, pp. 288-92; Jung 1966, pp. 69-71.
19. Budés letter for Longeuil, in Delaruelle 1907, p. 106; Gnoli 1891, pp. 12-28 (the opposing arguments in the appendix); Simar 1911, pp. 62-74; P. A. Becker 1924, pp. 21—35, 94—98; Renaudet 1954, pp. 202—203.
20. Simone 1949, pp. 38, 176; Saulnier 1951, pp. 2 ff; Le Goff 1964.
21. Alcalà opened in 1508. The polyglot Bible was completed there between 1514 and 1517. Louvain's Trilingual College was founded in 1517. Erasmus praised it in letters to Budé, although later in life he complained about difficulties at Louvain (*Opus Epistolarum*, letters nos. 689 and 778 to Budé; and nos. 1066,

1073 to others). Francis I intended to open a college for Greek studies in Milan, but he became so absorbed with other matters that the school was never opened. Its realization would have duly antagonized the Italians, who had their own Greek Centers; it would have drawn students and teachers away from the promised Collège de France. In the meantime, the plan delayed its opening: see Lefranc 1893, vol. I, p. 270.

22. Delaruelle 1907a, p. 132; on Budé's politico-patriotic digressions, pp. 161-67; for his alternating praise and blame of his countrymen, pp. 171-77.

22a. Budé letter to Erasmus, *Opus Epistolarum*, no. 522; La Garanderie 1967, p. 99.

23. In several letters Erasmus complains about the overabundance of invitations that he receives from all parts of Europe (*Opus Epistolarum*, nos. 794, 809, 1412). He was clearly less attracted by the French court than by the emperor, Charles V, whose subject he was and wanted to remain (nos. 778, 1432). In a letter to Budé (La Garanderie 1967, p. 247), Erasmus alleges that dire presentiments have kept him from moving to France. And in another letter (p. 260), he tells Budé outright that he never seriously considered settling there.

24. *Opus Epistolarum*, no. 522 (La Garanderie 1967, p. 102): "I love my country exceedingly . . . and I uphold my Frenchmen passionately"; or in no. 1812 (Fr. trans., pp. 254-55), his bitter complaints about Erasmus' flippant remarks on France.

24a. For the host of French humanists' attitudes toward Italy, see Mönch 1936, pp. 187-289; Simone 1949 and 1961, pp. 49-54; Busson 1957, p. 157, where the high water mark of intellectual influx is placed around 1530.

25. Budé [1524], preface; Delaruelle 1907a, p. 132.

26. Delaruelle 1907a. pp. 132, 230 annex II.

27. Reprinted in Weinberg 1950, pp. 77-80.

28. Barrillon 1897-99, vol. I, p. 119.

29. Dolet 1540, p. 29. I was unable to find any reference elsewhere to a speech by the king at Marignan.

30. On legendary origins: Kurth 1893, pp. 505 ff, and 1919, vol. I, pp. 52-65; Johannet 1923, pp. 38-42; Darmesteter and Hatzfeld 1923, pp. 71-74; Koht 1946-47, pp. 271-77, where the casual mode of inventing national legends is well described; Gerighausen 1963, 54-62; Huppert 1965; Jung 1966; Asher 1969, pp. 409-17; Dubois 1972 came too late to my attention for adequate utilization here.

31. Hotman 1972, pp. 197, 199.

32. Pasquier 1633, bk. I, chs. VI and XIV. Pasquier was apparently undecided whether to deprive his readers of the accustomed fable, and so, after condemning it on one page, he speaks confidently on the next about the defeat of the Trojans in connection with French history, or about the "first Trojan king," only to sweep it aside once more at the end of the chapter (chs. XIV, XV). He accepted, as did many of his fellow historians, the imaginary King Pharamond (bk. I, ch. VII; bk. 3, ch. VII).

33. Doubters of the Trojan past are included among most authors cited in note 30.

34. Connan 1609, vol. 2, ch. 9. pp. 145-46.

35. Bodin 1945, pp. 347-53.

36. Haillan 1615, vol. I, letter to the king and p. 21. Haillan devoted an entire chapter to "Pharamond Roy," (vol. I, pp. 1-13).

37. Pasquier 1633, bk. I, ch. I. Notice the many loving remarks about "my France," "our France," "this France."

38. Bodin 1945, pp. 344, 355, 356, 360.

39. Périon 1555, dedication to the king and dialogue II, in particular.

40. Pasquier, bk. 8, ch. 2, p. 677.

41. Picard 1556. See Dubois 1972, pp. 47 ff.

42. Secret 1969, pp. 123 ff.
43. *Liber de moribus veterum gallorum.* According to Waddington (1855, p. 457), the work had four Latin and two French editions. Waddington quotes (p. 232) a letter that Ramus wrote in 1571 where he says that "as the Gauls possessed all liberal arts in their own language before Ceasar's arrival, it is probable that today's Gauls still have their share of Gallic wisdom." There appears to be no trace of any wisdom the ancients had to learn from the Gauls in Ramus' scientific work, which is filled with references to the ancient sources.
44. Waddington 1855, p. 157.
45. Dubois 1972, with an edition of a treatise by G. Postel. Despite his sporadic francomania, I have omitted Postel for two reasons. One is that Postel's reasoning escapes my understanding. The other is that he was only occasionally enamored of the predominance of a French king in his scheme of things. Elsewhere he is quite willing to confer domination of the world to rulers of other nations.
46. Johannet 1923, pp. 37 ff; Chamard 1939-40, vol. 3, pp. 95-97.
47. Martin 1939, pp. 30,.338, for the self-centeredness of the French Church.
48. *Les Libertéz de l'Eglise gallicane.* 1594.
49. The *Traité* was written in 1594, according to an indication in the table of contents in the 1703 edition of Coquille's *Oeuvres.* The *Traité* covers pp. 75-91 in vol. 1. The observation on the Frankish origin occurs in vol. 1, pp. 418-19.
49a. An important exception to this observation is François Hotman, who, besides a German family background, had his religio-political reasons for insisting on the Germanic sources of French institutions.
50. Clément (1899) examines Estienne's contribution to the language (especially pp. 189-92, 224 ff). Nationalism in the field of grammar has been treated by Kukenheim 1932, ch. 5; Brunot 1966-1972, vol. 2, pp. 91 ff.
51. Estienne 1958, pp. 24-25. The infatuation with Greek ancestry continued, it seems, beyond the sixteenth century. See Brunot 1966-72, vol. 1, pp. 2-3 and n. 7; Gerighausen 1963, pp. 41, 70-101, for the seventeenth and eighteenth centuries. The French struggle to establish for themselves a non-Germanic origin went right into the eighteenth century: Johannet 1923, pp. 41-42.
52. Estienne 1850, pp. 1-3.
53. Chamard 1904, pp. 7-10, for the eulogizers of the French language before, pp. 10-15, and after the *Défense.*
54. Fauchet 1938 (1581), p. 25. Fauchet too worked "for the glory of the French name" (foreword addressed to the king).
55. Brunot 1966-72, vol 2, p. 13.
56. Chamard 1939-40, pp. 168 ff.
57. Spitzer 1954, p. 138.
58. Blignières 1851, p. 386.
59. Dolet 1540, p. 77, preface addressed "Au peuple françois."
60. Amyot 1559, dedication.
61. Belleforest 1566, dedication.
62. Gundesheimer 1966, pp. 90 ff. I have used Gundesheimer's translations.
63. Murarasu 1928, pp. 6, 110-11, 115, 139-40, 166.
64. MacFarlane 1959, p. 322. "Ad poetas gallicos."
65. Chamard 1939-40, pp. 168-71.
66. Murarasu 1928, p. 6.
67. Ronsard and Du Bellay, probably more often quoted and treated than any of their contemporary fellow poets, offer prime examples of the cohabitation in the same soul of love for the native province and love and praise for the common country.
68. Ronsard 1887-93, vol. 3, pp. 520-36.

69. We may argue whether Ronsard's self-contradictory thoughts expressed in this preface are due to divergent allegiances to Latin and French or to personal problems connected with the fate of the *Franciad,* or simply to what A. H. Becker (1896, p. 313) said about all sixteenth-century writers: namely, that they were capable of every abnegation except that of the mind, which is concision.
70. Aulotte 1965, with notes to contemporary exhortations in the same vein.
71. Pasquier 1633, vol. 1, no. 2, cols. 3-8.
72. How nationalism fared in the inflamed atmosphere of the civil wars has been treated recently and in an exemplary fashion by M. Yardeni in her *Conscience nationale en France pendant les guerres de religion* (1971). See also review in *Bibliothèque d'Humanisme et Renaissance* 1972, pp. 593-95.

ENGLAND

1. In a more concentrated form, the same national consciousness is expressed in the same play by another person, the exiled Bolinbroke, who laments:
    Then England's ground, farewell sweet soil, adieu;
    My mother and my nurse, that bears me yet.
    When e'er I wander, boast of this I can,
    Though banished, yet a true-born Englishman.
    [act 1, scene 3]
    And similar in feeling is this stanza from Spenser's *Faerie Queene:*
    Deare Countrey! O! how dearely deare
    Ought thy remembrance and perpetuall bond
    Be to thy foster Childe, that from thy hand
    Did commun breath and nouriture receave,
    How brutish is it not to understand
    How much to her we owe, that all us gave,
    That gave unto us all what ever good we have.
    [bk. 2, canto 10, stanza 69]
2. Percy 1966, pp. 103-106 passim; Levine 1973, pp. 40, 69-72, 76-79, 99-106; Loades 1974, pp. 184, 187; H. M. Smith 1862, pp. 200-201.
3. Morris (1967, pp. 39-48, 122, 154-55) says that England was backwards in all arts with the exception of music (p. 16); that England was mostly lucky: if she had been less despised, more feared, she might not have been allowed to survive (p. 40). D. C. Allen 1941, pp. 111, 143: England not as keen as the continent in the matter of astrology, whether in arguments for or against it. Fisher 1906, p. 216: All refined artifices were imported, and merchants and bankers were mostly Italians. Nef 1934-35, p. 23: Industrial methods began to evolve in England only in the second half of the century. Previously, "Great Britain was, industrially, in a backwater compared with Italy, Spain, the Low Countries, the South-German states, and even France. Englishmen had almost nothing to teach foreigners in the way of practical mechanical knowledge." In 1541, the French ambassador, Charles de Marillac, wrote to his king that foreign residents in England were being threatened with expulsion, although the English, who, he says, like to eat but not to work, need them badly, since they are "so ignorant in all mechanical skills that they cannot do without foreigners, however much they dislike them." (Marillac 1885, pp. 303-304, letter of 22 May 1541).

Modern English critics of the sixteenth century often remark on the lack of original theoretical thought in England, as, for instance, Morris 1953, introduction; Fussner 1970, p. 234; *The New Cambridge History* (G. R. Elton), vol. 2, p. 436; Bennett 1952, pp. 123-58. On English architecture, see Summerson 1970.

Henry VIII's court "photographer" was Hans Holbein the Younger, born in Augsburg. Also strangely backwards were English methods of execution, if we may believe travelers' reports: see Gurney-Salter 1930, p. 110, or Rye 1865, p. 89. As a matter of fact, for Anne Boleyn's decapitation, a French executioner, who did smart work with his sword, was imported, whereas the next queen to be executed, Catherine Howard, was disposed of with an axe, "according to the custom of the land," wrote Marillac (1885, p. 389) Mary Stuart, much later, was also butchered with an axe: see Maxwell-Stuart 1905, 208-9, 241. Most surprising is England's late awakening to long-distance seafaring: see Hakluyt 1903-1905, dedicatory epistle in vol. 1, p. xviii; Parks 1961, introduction, p. xiii; Quinn 1965, p. 51; Mattingly 1959, 397-99; Morison 1971, p. 273; Froude 1896, pp. 3, 9.

4. The contortions of the Henrician period have been described particularly well in H. M. Smith 1862, and in Scarisbrick 1968, especially ch. 10, "The Royal Supremacy." A contemporary witness, the French ambassador, Marillac, again writes to his king: "In respect to religion, they change their minds so often that I honestly cannot see the issue of the whole affair. Last year, they put to death those whom they had used before to clean out the monks and to appropriate their foundations for the king's benefit" (Marillac 1885, pp. 301-302).

5. Fabyan 1516, prologue, stanza 8.

6. Bale and Leylande 1549, fol. C lv-J 4v.

7. Hay 1950, p. xxxi, about this Italian historian's rejection of Arthur, and the attacks upon him. Bale, for one, says of Vergil that he is "polluting our English chronicles most shamefully with his Romish lies and other Italian beggaries." (Bale 1849 (1544), preface). Also Hay 1952, pp. 157 ff; Koebner 1953, pp. 31-46; Haller 1963, p. 63; A. B. Ferguson 1968, pp. 186-88, and 1969-70, pp. 23 ff, about that English humanist who rejected Brutus and Arthur but instead suggested a Phoenician ancestry for Britain; F. J. Levy 1967, pp. 125-30; Fussner 1970, pp. 252 ff; McKisack 1971, pp. 97-104. The most thorough study of the whole matter up to his time of writing (1922) is Hans Matter's *Englische Gründungssagen von Geoffrey of Monmouth bis zur Renaissance* (685 pp.).

8. Chapuys 1531 (reprint 1965), no. 45, Chapuys to Charles, pp. 19-20. In *Early English Text Society*, no. 17 pp. 199 ff, Henry quotes a Brutus fable in order to substantiate England's right to Scotland; Koebner 1953, pp. 40 ff. Edward VI's use of Brutus for England's rights over Scotland, in Matter 1922, pp. 490-91. Elizabeth too helped herself to a fable—in her case, to Joseph of Arimathias—in her answer to the Catholic bishops, who had humbly requested the Queen to return to the old faith: see Strype 1824, vol. 1, pp. 146-47 (reprint 1968, vol. 1, p. 218).

9. The legend began, apparently, in the thirteenth century with William of Malmesbury's *De antiquitate*. Foxe (1837-41, vol. 1, pp. 293, 312) writes without hesitation that Constantine was born in England. He also mentions the emperor's mother as an Englishwoman. Also Koebner 1953, pp. 31-46; Haller 1963, p. 63, quoting Bale's historical mythology; Loades 1970, pp. 28 ff, about Christian rewriting of history.

10. Bale 1810 (1553?), fol. B 4v (reprint in Oldys 1808-11, vol. 6, pp.

443-44); Parker 1605, p. 1; *EETS* 1871 (reprint 1969), "Joseph of Arimathias . . . an alliterative poem"; Winterhagen 1934, pp. 22 ff. The legend has also been scrutinized for possible truth in modern England: Cumings "On Joseph of Arimathea" (1878); Ravencroft's "The Coming of St. Joseph of Arimathias to England" (1928); and Dobson's "Did Our Lord Visit Britain?" (1944), where it is suggested that Christ might have visited England during the obscure years of his life and that Joseph of Arimathias might have come with him, possibly on business in the tin trade. L. S. Lewis, in *St. Joseph of Arimathias* (1954), concludes his investigation with these words: "How much harder to reject than to accept with awe and thankfulness the beautiful Arimathean tradition."

11. Royal and Protestant propaganda: Siebert 1952; Morris 1953, pp. 3-4; J. W. Allen 1951, pp. 124-33; Neale 1958, p. 9; Pineas 1968, pp. 214-21; Loades 1970, pp. 26-30, 260, and 1974, pp. 164-69.

12. Two striking examples: The rebels of the "Pilgrimage of Grace" of 1536 demanded, among other things, that Henry's legitimate daughter, Mary Tudor, bastardized by Henry's several acts of succession, be legitimized again because they feared that the crown might be handed over to a foreign prince. "Indeed, their primary dynastic objective apparently was to ensure the continuance of Tudors on the throne": Levine 1962 and 1973, pp. 157-58, document no. 20; Loades 1974, p. 184. The other occasion was the brief interruption of the legitimate succession to the throne after Edward VI's death, when Jane Grey, a Protestant, was to be substituted for the Catholic Mary: "The nation, resolved to have a true Tudor, acclaimed Mary": *The New Cambridge History*, vol. 2, p. 246; Levine 1962, p. 88, on how foreign diplomats misjudged the mood of the country: Loades 1974, p. 221, makes the same observation.

13. The Protestants were apparently in the minority for quite a while: "While English religion was predominantly Catholic in 1520, it had become predominantly Protestant well before 1600," A. G. Dickens 1965, p. 44. Loades 1965a, p. 62, and 1970, pp. 94-95.

14. Henry's elder sister Marguerite had been married to James IV of Scotland. However, Henry excluded the elder and more legitimate line from the succession to the throne to favor the line of his younger sister Mary, in case his three children should die without issue: see Levine 1962, document no. 23, and 1966, pp. 42-44, about the anti-Stuart feelings expressed in the 1562 play *Gorboduc*.

Ralph Sadler's parliamentary speech of 1565 is haunted by fear—and hatred—at the thought of accepting Mary Queen of Scots as his possible English Queen: ". . . The nature of Englishmen has always so much detested the regiment of strangers that they have made laws to bar all titles which a stranger may claim of inheritance within the realm." A Scot, he says, once told him that Scotland would never tolerate an English king, that the common people and the stones in the street would rise against him. And even so, Sadler goes on, "the English common people and the stones in the street would rebel against [a Scot]" (Sadler 1809, vol. 3, pp. 323-27).

One of the most emotional pieces against Mary Stuart might easily be the document no. 33, reprinted in part in Levine 1973, p. 180: "Mary Queen of Scots' claim to the English succession attacked on National and Religious Grounds," 1565. Here we hear that the Scots are "a people by custom and almost nature our enemies, thirsty of blood, poor and miserable. . . . Corrupt religion, blinded with the hate of the truth of the gospel . . . has induced so many to affect the Queen of Scots in this case of succession . . . so that they might once more turn unto their accustomed idolatry and wonted crueltry to wash their hands in the blood of the faithful. . . ."

15. In a pamphlet of 1554, Knox had already branded Mary as "an open traitress to the Imperial Crown of England [by bringing] . . . a stranger and [making] a proud Spaniard king": Percy 1966, p. 153. Dickens (1965, p. 54) stresses the profit for Protestantism gained through Mary's zealotry: "She . . . identified Catholicism with unpopular Spain." Loades (1965, p. 247) speaks of the practically universal resistance to Philip, especially among "the parliamentarian gentry, whose stubborn resistance . . . had finally wrecked the alliance . . . . These gentlemen from 1558 onward became the backbone of English nationalism."

16. Fol. D vii–viii of Morison's *Exhortation*, reprinted in Zeeveld 1948, p. 233.

17. Latimer 1855, p. 385.

18. Latimer 1844, p. 91.

19. *The New Cambridge History*, vol. 2, p. 245.

20. Foxe 1837–41, vol. 6, pt. 1, p. 152; Fuller 1845, vol. 4, p. 119.

21. Loades 1970, pp. 22 ff; Olsen 1973, p. 58, about the martyrs seeing themselves as actors in the great Christian drama; Haller 1963, on how persecution' confirmed· the victims' assurance at their election.

22. The sensational success of the *Book of Martyrs*, or *Acts and Monuments*, is mentioned in every study on Foxe.

23. Loades 1974, p. 246 ff, for the success of Protestants as the result of five years of persecution. Olsen (1973) warns of reading narrow nationalism into Foxe's book. Yet Foxe speaks very frequently as an Englishman, when he says, for instance, that Wycliffe was "our countryman . . . whom the Lord . . . raised up here in England to detect . . . the poison of the pope's doctrine" (Foxe 1837–41, vol. 2. pt. 2, p. 791), or when he judges Mary's reign and remarks that she unnecessarily brought King Philip into the country "and by her strange marriage with him [made] the whole of England subject unto a stranger" (Foxe, vol. 7, pt. 2, pp. 626–27).

24. So Foxe calls Elizabeth in his dedication of the first English edition of his work (Ibid., vol. 1, "Preface" no. vii). Elizabeth, like Constantine, Foxe explains, had ended the persecution of the faithful.

25. Aylmer 1559, fol. P 4r.

26. Ibid., fol. P 4v.

27. Parker 1853, p. 419.

28. *Euphues and His England*, p. 434.

29. Ibid., pp. 439–40.

30. Quoted in Neale 1958, p. 11.

31. Hakluyt 1903–1905, vol. 8, p. 36, "Report of the voyages . . . attempted in . . . 1583 by Sir Humfrey Gilbert . . . written by M. Edward Haie . . . ," pp. 34–77; Quinn 1940, vol. 2, p. 387, and 1965, p. 236.

32. Davys 1595 (reprint 1812), pp. 66–67; Raleigh 1910, pp. 48–49; Wright 1970, pp. 329–52, "The Elect of God." Lest it be thought that such religious self-righteousness was typically English, the following text will show that the same had been said much earlier in Spain: A Dr. Pedro de Santander wrote to his king, Philip II, in 1557 to assure him that "It is lawful that your Majesty like a good shepherd, appointed by the hand of the Eternal Father, should tend and lead out your sheep, since the Holy Spirit has.shown spreading pastures whereupon are feeding lost sheep which have been snatched away by the . . . Demon. These pastures are the New World . . . now in possession of the Demon. . . . This is the land promised by the Eternal Father to the faithful, since we are commanded by God in the Holy Scriptures to take it from them,

108 | NOTES

being idolaters, and [at this point the conquistador's nature takes over] by reason of their idolatry and sin to put them all to the knife, leaving no living thing save maidens and children; their cities robbed and sacked, their walls and houses levelled to the earth." Quoted in Parkman 1897–1901, vol. 1, p. 18, n. 2. The original letter, more than twenty pages long, can be found in *Colección de documentos*, vol. 26, p. 355. According to Sanford (1961, p. 49), the conquistadors "almost without exception, considered themselves divinely appointed to gain glory for Spain in the New World." Wright 1943.

33. Harrison 1878, vol. 1, pp. 77, 129–30. But warnings against traveling to a vice-ridden country like Italy were frequent, and were part of the anti-Italian moralizing, Protestant, often obstreperous self-assertiveness and xenophobia. Cf. Parks 1961a.
34. Harrison 1878, vol. 1, p. 155.
35. Ibid., pp. 150–51.
36. *Euphues*, p. 425.
37.· Ibid., p. 423.
38. Camden 1806 (1607), 1590, 1594 editions, fols. Av–A 3v.
39. On Camden and his work: Levy 1964; Piggot 1951; Trevor-Roper 1971, pp. 8–9.
40. Notes to Thomas 1861, p. 113.
41. Hooper 1843, p. 468.
42. Ponet 1942, p. 61.
43. Bradbrook 1953, pp. 59–60, 65.
44. Rankins 1585, p. 2.
45. Greene 1881–86, vol. 2, pp. 226–27.
46. Morley 1971, pp. 77–78.
47. Hoby 1928 (1561), pp. 1–5.
48. Pettie 1581, p. 10, "To the Reader."
49. Ibid., pp. 9–11.
50. Wilson 1553 (reprint 1967), pp. 183–84.
51. Kermode and Hollander 1973, vol. 1; G. G. Smith 1904.
52. Ascham, it is true, is a weak representative for English-written literature. In his *Toxophilus* (1545), he explains at length what made him renounce "my profit and name" and write in English (pp. xiii–xiv). While he no longer apologizes in his *Scholemaster* (posthumously published in 1570), his interest in the English language is far from overwhelming, since this work was intended as a "plain and perfect way of teaching children to understand, write, and speak the Latin tongue, but specially purposed for the private bringing up of youth in gentlemen and noblemen's houses, and commodious for all such as have forgotten the Latin tongue and would themselves... recover a sufficient hability to understand, write, and speak Latin." (The foregoing is the title of the book: p. 182 of Ascham 1970.)
53. Mozley 1940, p. 136.
54. Mulcaster 1582 (reprint 1970), p. 254.

Bibliography

A

Acton, John Emerich Edward Dalberg. 1907. *The History of Freedom and Other Essays.* London. (First published 1862 in *Home and Foreign Review.*)

Albèri, Eugenio. 1839-1863. *Relazioni degli ambasciatori veneti al senato.* 15 vols. Florence.

Alberti, F. L. 1553. *Descrizione di tutta Italia.* Venice.

Allen, Don Cameron. 1941. *The Star-Crossed Renaissance. The Quarrel about Astrology and its Influence in England.* Durham,

Allen, J. W. 1951. *A History of Political Thought in the Sixteenth Century.* 3d ed London.

Allut, P. 1859. *Etude biographique et bibliographique sur Symphorien Champier (1472-1539?).* Lyon.

Allworth, Edward, ed. 1971. *Soviet Nationality Problems.* New York-London.

———. 1971a. *Nationalities of the Soviet East: Publications and Writing Systems. A Bibliographical Directory and Transliteration Tables for Iranian and Turkic-Language Publications, 1818-1945, Located in U. S. Libraries.* New York.

Almeida, Fortunato de. 1922-1929. *Historia de Portugal.* 6 vols in 5. Coimbra.

Ammirato, Scipio. 1599. *Discorsi sopra Cornelio Tacito.* Brescia.

Amyot, Jacques. 1559. *Les vies des hommes illustres grecs et romains, comparées, . . . translatées du grec en françois.* Paris.

Angermeier, Heinz. 1956. Begründung und Inhalt der Reichsreform. *Zeitschrift der Savigny Stiftung für Reichsgeschichte, Germanistische Abteilung* 75: 181-205.

Ansheim, V., 1888. *Die Berner Chronik,* vols. 3-4. Bern.

Antologia portuguesa. Paladinos de linguagem. See under Campos 1922-1926.

Arco, Ricardo del. 1939. *Fernando el Católico. Artificio de la España imperial.* Saragossa.

Ariosto, Lodovico. 1968. *Orlando Furioso,* translated by W. St. Rose. New York.

Arnold, Klaus. 1971. *Johann Trithemius (1462-1516).* Würzburg.

Ascham, Roger, 1970. *English Works: Tolophilus. Report of the Affairs and State of Germany. The Scholemaster,* edited by William Aldis Wright. Reprint ed. Cambridge.

Asher, R. A. 1969. Myth, Legend and History in Renaissance France. *Studi Francesi* 13: 409-419.

Astraín, A. 1912-1920. *Historia de la Compañía de Jesús en la asistencia de España.* 6 vols. 2d ed. Madrid.

Aubin, Hermann. 1938. *Von Raum und Grenzen des deutschen Volkes,* vol. 6. Breslauer Historische Forschungen. Breslau.

Aulotte, Robert. 1965. Une défense manuscrite de la langue francaise au XVIe siècle. *Bibliothèque d'Humanisme et Renaissance* 27: 513-22.

Aylmer, John. 1559. *An Harborowe for Faithful and trewe subjectes . . . .* Strassburg.

B

Bader, Karl Siegf. 1954. Kaiser und ständischer Reformgedanke in der Reichsreform des endenden 15. Jahrhunderts. *Historisches Jahrbuch* 73: 74-94. Munich.

Baguenault de Puchesse, Fernand. 1912. Un Projet de candidature de Henri IV au trône impérial. *Séances et Travaux de l'Académie des Sciences morales et politiques* (Institut de France) 177: 639-50. Paris.

Bale, John. 1810. The Vocacyon of Johan Bale to the Bishoprick of Ossorio in Ireland . . . . *The Harleian Miscellany, a Collection of Scarce, Curious, and Entertaining Pamphlets and Tracts,* vol. 6. London.

———. 1849. Chronicle of the Examination &

Death of Lord Cobham (1544). In *Selected Works of John Bale*. Parker Society, vol. 35. Cambridge, Eng.

Bale, John, and Leylande, John. 1549. *The Laboryous Journey of J. L. for Englandes Antiquitees*. London.

Baron, Hans. 1955. *The Crisis of the Early Italian Renaissance*. 2 vols. Princeton.

———. 1968. Imitation, Rhetoric and Quattrocento Thought in Bruni's 'Laudatio'. *Francesco Petrarca to Leonardo Bruni. Studies in Humanistic and Political Literature*. Chicago-London.

Barrès, Maurice. 1965-1968. Traits éternels de la France. In *L'Oeuvre de Maurice Barrès*, vol. 8. Paris.

Barillon, Jean. 1897-1899. *Journal de Jean Barillon, secrétaire du chancelier Duprat*, edited by P. de Vaissière. 2 vols. Paris.

Baruzi, J. 1922. Le Problème des citations scripturaires en langue latine dans l'oeuvre de St. Jean de la Croix. *Bulletin Hispanique* 24: 18-40.

Bataillon, Marcel. 1924. Erasme et la Chancellerie impériale. *Bulletin Hispanique* 3: 27-34.

———. 1925. Honneur et Inquisition. *Bulletin Hispanique* 27: 5-17.

———. 1930. Du Nouveau sur J. L. Vives. *Bulletin Hispanique* 32: 97-113.

———. 1937. *Erasme et l'Espagne*. Paris.

———. 1952. *Etudes sur le Portugal au temps de l'humanisme*. Coimbra.

Beau. A. E. 1937. Nation und Sprache im portugiesischen Humanismus. *Volkstum und Kultur der Romanen* 10: 65-82.

Bebel, Heinrich, 1509. *Opera Bebeliana*. Frankfurt.

———. 1727. *Rerum Suevicarum Scriptores*. Collection Goldast. Frankfurt.

Becker, A. Henri. 1896. *Un Humaniste au XVIe siecle: Loys Le Roy de Coutance* [Ludovicus Regius]. Paris.

Becker, Philipp A. 1924. *Christophle de Longueil, sein Leben und sein Brief-Wechsel*. Bonn-Leipzig.

Bell, Aubrey F. G. 1925. *Luis de León*. Oxford.

———. 1941. Damião de Goes, A Portuguese Humanist. *Hispanic Review* 9: 243-51.

Belleforest, Francois. 1566. *Les Epistres familières de Marc Tulle Ciceron . . . traduites de latin en françoys . . . partie par E. Dolet et le reste par F. de Belleforest*. Paris.

Belli, Pierno. 1936. *De re militari et bello tractatus*, translated by H. C. Nutting. [Latin and English en face.] Oxford-London.

Benjamin, Edwin B. 1959. Fame, Poetry, and the Order of History in the Literature of the English Renaissance. *Studies in the Renaissance* 6: 64-84.

Bennett, H. S. 1952. *English Books and Readers, 1475-1557*. Cambridge, Eng.

Berges, Wilhelm. 1952. Das Reich ohne Hauptstadt. In *Festgabe zum 90. Geburtstag von Friedrich Meinecke, Jahrbuch der Geschichte des deutschen Ostens*, vol. 1. Tübingen.

Bieder, Theobald. 1939. *Geschichte der Germanenforschung 1500-1806*. 2d ed. Leipzig.

Bierlaire, Franz. 1968. *La Familia d'Erasme. Contribution à l'histoire de l'humanisme*. Paris.

Birch, Edward, T. 1749. *An Historical View of the Negotiations between the Courts of England, France, and Brussels from the year 1592 to 1617, extracted chiefly from the MS. State Papers of Sir Thomas Edmondes . . . drawn up by Sir George Carew . . . from his embassy there in 1609*. London.

Blignières, Auguste de. 1851. *Essai sur Amyot*. Paris.

Bloch, Marc. 1924. *Les Rois thaumaturges. Etude sur le caractère surnaturel attribué à la puissance royale, particulièrement en France et en Angleterre*. Strassburg.

———. 1949. *La Société féodale*. Bibliothèque de synthèse historique. Paris.

———. 1961. *Feudal Society*, translated by L. A. Manyon. Chicago.

Boas, George. 1969. *Vox Populi: Essays in the History of an Idea*. Baltimore.

Bodin, Jean. 1576. *Les Six livres de la République de Jean Bodin Angevin*. Paris.

———. 1945. *Method for the Easy Comprehension of History*, translated by B. Reynolds. New York.

———. 1967. *Six Books of the Commonwealth;* translated by M. J. Tooley (abridged). Reprinted. New York.

Boehmer, Heinrich. 1928. *The Jesuits*, translated by Paul Z. Strodach. Philadelphia.

Boiardo, Matteo-Maria. 1580. *Orlando Innamorato*. Venice.

Bornate, Carlo, ed. [1915]. *Mercurino Arborio di Gattinara, Cardinale, 1465-1530: Historia vite et gestorum. . . .* [Turin].

Boulenger, Jacques. 1934. Le Vrai siècle de la Renaissance. *Humanisme et Renaissance* 1: 9-30.

Bourdon, A. A. 1970. *Histoire du Portugal*. Paris.

Bowen, Willis B. 1950. Sixteenth-Century French Translations of Machiavelli. *Italica* 4: 313-19.

Bradbrook, M. C. 1953. *The Queen's Garland, Verses Made by her Subjects for Elizabeth I, Queen of England, Collected in Honour of Her Majesty Queen Elizabeth II*. Oxford.

Brandi, Karl. 1937. *Kaiser Karl V. Werden und Schicksal einer Persönlichkeit und eines Weltreiches*. Munich.

Brown, Harcourt. 1960. The Renaissance

and Historians of Science. *Studies in the Renaissance* 7: 27-42.

Brunot, Ferdinand. 1966-1972. *Histoire de la langue francaise des origines à nos jours.* 21 vols. Reprint of the 4th ed. Paris.

Buchholtz, F. B. von. 1831-38. *Geschichte der Regierung Ferdinand I.* 9 vols. Vienna.

Buck, August. 1952. *Italienische Dichtungslehren.* Tübingen.

Budé, Guillaume. [1524]. *De Asse et partibus eius libri 5.* Paris.

———. 1520. *De contemptu rerum fortuitarum libri 3.* [Paris].

Burdach, Konrad, and Piur, P., 1913-1928. Rienzo und die geistige Wandlung seiner Zeit. *Briefwechsel des Cola di Rienzo. Vom Mittelalter zur Reformation, pt. 1,* vol. 2. Berlin.

Bush, Douglas. 1956. *The Renaissance and English Humanism.* Toronto.

Busson, Henri. 1957. *Le Rationalisme dans la littérature française de la Renaissance (1533-1601).* Paris.

Butterfield, H. 1959. History of Science and the Study of History. *Harvard Library Bulletin* 13: 329-47.

C

Cambridge University Press. 1957-1970. *The New Cambridge Modern History.* 14 vols. Cambridge, Eng.

Camden, William. 1806. *Britannia, or a Chorographical Description of the Flourishing Kingdom of England, Scotland, and Ireland . . . .* 4 vols. (The 1607 ed., enlarged and translated by R. Gough.) 2d ed. London.

Camões, Luis de. 1950. *The Lusiads,* translated by L. Bacon. [Originally published 1572.] N. Y.

Campos, Agostinho da, ed. 1922-1926. *Antologia portuguesa: Paladinos de linguagem,* 3 vols. (1st vol. is a 2d ed.). Paris-Lisbon.

Cardascia, G. 1943. Machiavelli et Jean Bodin. *Bibliographie d'Humanisme et Renaissance* 3: 129-76.

Cassirer, Ernst. 1955. *The Myth of the State.* Garden City, N. Y.

Castiglione, Baldassare. 1894. *Il Cortigiano,* edited by V. Cian. Florence.

Castro, Amerigo. 1931. *Cervantès.* Paris.

Celtis, Conrad. 1518. *Urbis Norimberbergae Conradi Celtis . . . de origine, situ, moribus et institutis descriptio.* Nuremberg.

———. 1943. *Germania generalis,* edited by F. Pindter. Leipzig.

Cervantès, Miguel de. 1917-1923. *Obras completas.* vol. 7. Facs. of 1st eds. Madrid.

Chabod, Federico. 1967. *Scritti sul Rinascimento.* Turin.

Chamard, Henri. 1904. *Joachim Du Bellay, La Défense et l'Illustration de la langue française.* Paris.

———. 1939-1940. *Histoire de la Pléiade.* 4 vols. Paris.

Chapuys, Eustache. 1531. *Public Record Office. Calendar of Letters and Papers,* vol. 5. London 1880. Reprint Vaduz 1965.

Chevalier, Louis. 1958. *Classes laborieuses et classes dangereuses a Paris pendant la première moitié du XIXe siècle.* Paris.

Chevalier, Maxime. 1966. *L'Arioste en Espagne. 1530-1650. Recherche sur l'influence du "Roland Furieux."* Bordeaux.

Choulgine, Alex. 1937. *Les Origines de l'esprit national moderne et Jean-Jacques Rousseau.* Annales de la Société de J.-J. Rousseau, vol. 26. Geneva.

Church, Will. Farr. 1931. *Constitutional Thought in Sixteenth-Century France. A Study in the Evolution of Ideas.* Cambridge Mass. Reprint New York 1968.

Cian, Vittorio. 1911. Contro il volgare. In *Letterari e linguistici,* pp. 251-97. Milan.

———. 1936. La Coscienza nazionale nel Rinascimento. *Scritti minori,* pp. 143-73. Turin.

Cirot, Georges. 1905. *Mariana historien.* Paris.

Clément, Louis. 1899. *Henri Estienne et son oeuvre française.* Paris.

Cochrane, Eric. 1965. The End of the Renaissance in Florence. *Bibliothèque d'Humanisme et Renaissance* 27: 7-29.

Commynes, Philip de. 1924-25. *Mémoires.* 3 vols. Reprint Paris 1964-65.

Conley, C. H. 1967. *The First English Translators of the Classics.* New York.

Connan, Francois de Paris. 1609. Connani Francisci Parisiensis *Libri X, argumentis tum ante singolorum librorum capita.* Hanover.

Conrad, Hermann. 1962. *Deutsche Rechtsgeschichte.* 2 vols. 2d ed. Karlsruhe.

Coquille, Guy. 1650. *Oeuvres posthumes.* Paris.

———. 1703. *Les Oeuvres de maistre Guy Coquille.* 2 vols. Bordeaux.

Coreth, Anna. 1950. Dynastisch-politische Ideen Kaiser Maximilian I. *Mitteilungen des österreichischen Staatsarchivs* 3: 81-105.

Coulton, G. G. 1935-1937. Nationalism in the Middle Ages. *Cambridge Historical Journal* 5: 15-44.

Courcelle, Pierre. 1948. *Histoire littéraire des grandes invasions germaniques.* Paris.

Crinito, Pietro [1510]. *De honesta disciplina libri 25, de poetis latinis libri 5, et Poematum libri 2,* edited by C. Angeleri. Edizione nazionale dei classici del pensiero italiano, ser. 2. Rome 1955.

112 | BIBLIOGRAPHY

Cuming, H. S. 1878. On Joseph of Arimathea. *The Journal of the British Archaeological Association* 34: 182-86.

Curcio, S. 1934. *Dal Rinascimento alla Controriforma. Contributo alla storia del pensiero italiano, da Guicciardino a Botero.* Rome.

D

Dante. 1831. *Il Convito di Dante Alligheri,* edited by F. Pederzini et al. Modena.

Darmesteter, A., and Hatzfeld, A. 1923. *Le Seizième siècle en France. Tableau de la littérature et de la langue.* Paris.

Davys, John. 1595. The World's Hydrographical Description. *A Selection of Curious, Rare, and Early Voyages . . . Chiefly Published by Hakluyt but not Included in His Celebrated Compilation.* Reprint London 1812.

Delaruelle, Louis. 1907. *Répertoire analytique et chronologique de la correspondance de Guillaume Budé.* Toulouse. Reprint New York n. d.

———. 1907a. *Guillaume Budé, les origines, les débuts, les idées maîtresses.* Paris. Reprint Geneva 1970.

Deutsch, K. W. 1953. *Nationalism and Social Communication. An Inquiry into the Foundations of Nationality.* Boston-London.

Deutsche Reichtagsakten unter Karl V. 1962. 8 vols. 2d ed. (Vol. 1, edited by August Kluckhohn.) Göttingen.

———. 1972. Ibid., edited by Ernst Bock. 3 vols. Gottingen.

Dickens, A. G. 1965. The Reformation in England. In *The Reformation Crisis,* edited by Joel Hurstfield. New York.

Diehl, A. 1937. Heiliges römisches Reich deutscher Nation. *Historische Zeitschrift* 156: 457-84.

Dobson, C. C. 1944. Did our Lord Visit Britain as They Say in Cornwall and Somerset? *Destiny, The Magazine of National Life,* pp. 5-29.

Dolet, Estienne. 1536-1538. *Commentarii linguae latinae tomus primus et secundus.* 2 vols. Lyon.

———. 1540. *Les Gestes de Francois de Valois.* Lyon.

———. 1540a. *La Maniere de bien traduire d'une langue en l'aultre.* Lyon. [*See* Weinberg 1950.]

Dollmann, Eugen. 1927. *Die Probleme der Reichspolitik in den Zeiten der Gegenreformation und die politischen Denkschriften des Lazarus von Schwendi.* Munich.

Domenichi, Lodovico. 1549. *Rime diverse di molti eccelentissimi autori.* Venice.

Doni, A. F. 1928. *I Marmi,* edited by E. Chiòrboli, 2 vols. Bari.

Dotzauer, Winifred. 1966. Heinrich IV. von Frankreich und die Frage der römischen

Kaiserwahl. *Zeitschrift für die Geschichte des Oberrheins* n. s. 75: 71-146.

Doucet, R. 1948. *Les Institutions de la France au XVIe siècle.* 2 vols. Paris.

Douglas, David C. 1969. *The Norman Achievement.* London.

Druffel, August von. 1873-1882. *Briefe und Akten zur Geschichte des 16. Jahrhunderts* . . . . 3 vols. Munich.

Dubois, Claude-Gilbert. 1972. *Celtes et Gaulois au XVIe siècle. Le développement littéraire d'un mythe nationaliste. Avec l'édition critique d'un traité inédit de Guillaume Postel.* Paris.

Du Mont [Dumont], J. 1726-1731. *Corps diplomatique du droit des gens, contenant un recueil des traitez d'alliance, de paix, de trêve . . . depuis le règne de Charlemagne jusqu'à present.* 8 vols. and supp. Amsterdam.

Duplessis, Philippe de Mornay. 1824-1825. *Mémoires et correspondance. 1549-1623.* 17 vols. Paris.

Dupont-Ferrier, Gustave. 1940. Le Sens des mots *Patria* et *Patrie* en France au moyen âge et jusqu'au début du XVIIe siècle. *Revue historique* 188: 87-104.

Du Tillet, Jean. 1578. *Mémoires et recherches.* Rouen.

———. 1580. *Recueil des rois de France, leurs couronne et maisons.* Paris.

E

EETS: Early English Text Society. Original ser., 1871. Extra ser.. 1969. London.

Ehrenberg, Richard. [1928]. *Capital and Finances in the Age of the Renaissance. A Study of the Fuggers and their Connections.* Translated by H. M. Lucas. New York. [German ed. 1896, 2 vols.]

Eisenstein, Elizabeth L. 1966. Clio and Chronos. An Essay on the Making and Breaking of History-Book Time. *History and Theory. Studies in the Philosophy of History,* supp. 6: 36-64. The Hague.

Entwistle, W. J. 1947. Cervantes' Two Odes on the Invincible Armada. *Bulletin of Spanish Studies* 24: 254-59.

Erasmus. 1906-1958. *Opus Epistolarum Erasmi Roterodami.* 12 vols. Oxford.

Estienne, Henri. 1850. *La Précellence du langage francois,* edited by Léon Feugère. Paris.

———. 1958. *Traité de la conformité du langage francois avec le grec nouveau,* edited by Léon Feugère. Paris. Reprint Geneva 1970.

———. 1965. *Henricus Stephanus II, Francofordiense Emporium . . . anno 1574.* Amsterdam.

Eyck, F. G. 1955. The Political Theories and Activities of the German Academic Youth between 1815 and 1819. *The Journal of Modern History* 4: 27-38.

F

Fabian, Ekehart. 1962. *Die Entstehung des Schmalkaldischen Bundes und seiner Verfassung, 1524-1529, 1531-1535.* Schriften zur Kirchen- und Rechtsgeschichte. Tübingen.

Fabyan, R. 1516. *The New Chronicles of England and France in two parts, named by himself The Concord of Histories.* N. p.

Fauchet, Claude. 1938. *Recueil de l'origine de la langue et poésie françoises, rymes et romans,* edited by G. Espiner-Scott. Paris.

Febvre, L., and Martin, H.-M., 1955. *L'Apparition du livre.* L'Evolution humaine. Bibliothèque de Synthèse historique, vol. 49. Paris.

Feist Hirsch, Elisabeth. 1967. *Damião de Gois. The Life and Thought of a Portuguese Humanist, 1502-1574,* The Hague.

Ferguson, A. B. 1968. Circumstances and the Sense of History in Tudor England: The Coming of the Historical Revolution. *Medieval and Renaissance Series* 3: 170-205.

———. 1969, 1970. John Twyne: A Humanist and the Problem of Legend. *The Journal of British Studies* 9: 24-44.

Ferguson, William Scott. 1913. *Greek Imperialism.* Boston-New York.

Fichtenau, H. 1959. *Der junge Maximilian, 1459-1482.* Munich.

———. 1965. Reich und Dynastie im politischen Denken Maximilian I. In *Festgabe fur Hugo Hantsch: Österreich und Europa,* pp. 39-47. Graz-Vienna-Cologne.

Finke, Heinrich. 1916. *Weltimperialismus und nationale Regungen im späteren Mittelalter.* Freiburg-Leipzig.

Fischer-Galati, Stephen A. 1959. *Ottoman Imperialism and German Protestantism 1521-1555.* Cambridge, Mass.

Fisher, H. A. L. 1906. *The History of England from the Accession of Henry VII to the Death of Henry VIII, 1485-1547.* The Political History of England, 12 vols. Reprint New York 1969.

Folengo, Teofilo. 1953. *Il Baldus e le altre opere latine e volgari,* edited by U. E. Paoli. Florence.

Fondazione Treccani degli Alfieri. 1953-1966. *Storia di Milano,* vol. 7, edited by Gino Franceschini. Milan.

Fouqueray, H. 1910-1925. *Histoire de la Compagnie de Jésus en France, des origines à la suppression, 1528-1762.* 5 vols. Paris.

Foxe, John. 1837-1841. *The Acts and Monuments of John Foxe: a New and Complete edition with a preliminary dissertation by the Rev. George Townsend,* edited by the Rev. Stephen Cattley, 8 vols. London.

Fracastoro, Geronimo. 1813. *Della Sifilide.* Milan. [Italian and Latin en face.]

Franck, Sebastian. 1565. *Chronica: Zeytbuch und Geschichtbibel von Anbeginn . . . N. p.*

François, Michel. 1958. L'Idée d'Empire en France à l'époque de Charles Quint. In *Colloques internationaux du centre national de la recherche scientifique: Sciences humaines. Charles Quint.* Sept.-Oct.: 23-35.

Freising, Bishop Otto of, and Rahwein. 1965. *Die Taten Friedrichs, oder richtiger Cronica: gesta Frederici seu rectius cronica,* edited by G. Waitz and B. Simson; translated by A. Schmidt. Berlin. [Latin and German en face.]

Froude, J. A. 1896. *English Seamen in the Sixteenth Century.* London.

Fueter, E. 1919. *Geschichte des europäischen Staatensystems von 1492-1559.* Munich-Berlin.

Fuller, Thomas. 1845. *The Church History of Britain.* 6 vols. Oxford.

Fussner, F. S. 1970. *Tudor History and the Historians.* New York.

G

Gaetano, A. L. de. 1967. Gelli and the Rebellion against Latin. *Studies in the Renaissance* 14: 131-58.

Galbraith, V. H. 1941. Nationality and Language in Medieval England. *Transactions of the Royal Historical Academy* 23: 113-28.

Gerighausen, Joseph. 1963. *Die historische Deutung der Nationalsprache im französischen Schrifttum des 16. Jahrhunderts. Romanistische Versuche und Vorarbeiten, Romanisches Seminar.* Bonn.

Gerlich, Alois. 1960. *Habsburg-Luxemburg-Wittelsbach im Kampf um die deutsche Kaiserkrone. Studien zur Vorgeschichte des Königtums Ruprechts von der Pfalz.* Wiesbaden.

Giannotti, Donato. 1819. *Opere. Collezione de ottimi scrittori italiani,* vol. 3. Pisa.

———. 1850. *Opere,* edited by F. L. Polidori. 2 vols. Florence. [The "Discorso delle cose d'Italia" is in vol. 1, pp. 289-340.]

Gilbert, Felix. 1954. The Concept of Nationalism in Machiavelli's *Prince. Studies in the Renaissance,* vols. 1-5: 38-48.

——— 1965. Machiavelli and Guicciardini. *Politics and History in 16th-Century Florence.* Princeton.

Giovio, Paolo. 1931. *Le Vite del Gran Capitano e del Marchese Pescara,* translated by Ludovico Domenichi; edited by Constantine Panigada. Bari.

——— 1577. *Elogia virorum literis illustrium.* Basel.

Gnoli, D. 1891. *Un Giudizio di lesa romanità sotto Leone X.* Rome.

Godechot, Jacques. 1951. *Les Institutions de*

114 | BIBLIOGRAPHY

la France sous la Révolution et l'Empire. Paris.
———. 1963. Les Révolutions 1770-1799. Paris.
———. 1965. La Prise de la Bastille. Paris.
———. 1971. Nation, Patrie, Nationalisme et Patriotisme en France au XVIIe siècle. Annales historiques de la Révolution Francaise 43: 481-501.
Goetz, Walter. 1939. Das Werden des italienischen Nationalgefühls. Sitzungbericht der Bayerischen Akademie der Wissenschaft 7: 5-54.
Goetz, Werner. 1958. Translatio imperii. Ein Beitrag zur Geschichte des Geschichtsdenkens und der politischen Theorien im Mittelalter und in der frühen Neuzeit. Tübingen.
Goldast, Melchior. 1727. Rerum Svevicarum scriptores. 2d ed. Ulm.
Goldschmidt, E. P. 1943. Medieval Texts and Their First Appearance in Print. Bibliographical Society Transactions, supps. 11-17: 1-121. Oxford.
Gooch, G. P. 1920. Nationalism. London.
Gothein, Eberhard. 1878. Politische und religiöse Volksbewegung vor der Reformation. Breslau.
Granvelle, Cardinal de. 1841-1852. Papiers d'Etat du Cardinal de Granvelle. 9 vols. Collection de documents inédits sur l'histoire de France. Paris.
Grayson, C. 1960. Lorenzo, Machiavelli and the Italian Language. Italian Renaissance Studies. pp. 410-32. London.
Greene, Robert. 1881-1886. The Life and Works in Prose and Verse, edited by Alex B. Grosart. 15 vols. London-Aylesbury.
Grendler, Paul F. 1969. Critics of the Italian World (1530-1560). Anton Francesco Doni Nicolò Franco and Ortensio Lando. Madison-Milwaukee-London.
Grisar, Hartmann, S. J. 1927. Martin Luther und sein Werk. 2d ed. Freiburg.
Grosjean, Georges. 1927. Le Sentiment national dans la Guerre de Cent Ans. Paris.
Guicciardini, Francesco. 1953. Opere, edited by V. de Caprariis. Milan-Naples.
Gundsheimer, Werner L. 1966. The Life and Work of Louis le Roy. Travaux d Humanisme et Renaissance, vol. 82. Geneva.
Gurney-Salter, Emma. 1930. Tudor England through Venetian Eyes. London.
Guy, Alain. 1943. La Pensée de Fray 'Louis Léon. Limoges.

H

Haillan, Girard B. du. 1615. Histoire générale des rois de France (1584). 2 vols. Paris.
Hakluyt, Richard. 1903-1905. The Principall Navigations, Voyages, Traffiques and Discoveries of the English Nation. 12 vols. Glasgow.
Halbauer, Fritz. 1929. Mutianus Rufus und

seine geistesgeschichtliche Stellung. Beiträge zur Kulturgeschichte des Mittelalters und der Renaissance, vol. 38. Leipzig-Berlin.
Hale, J. R. 1965. The Early Development of the Bastion. An Italian Chronology, c. 1450-c. 1534. In Europe in the Late Middle Ages, edited by Hale et al. Evanston.
Hall, Vernon. 1945. Renaissance Literary Criticism. A Study of its Social Content. New York.
Haller, William. 1963. Foxe's Book of Martyrs and the Elect Nation. London.
Hallowell, Rob. E. 1962. Ronsard and the Gallic Hercules Myth. Studies in the Renaissance 9: 242-55.
Hanotaux, G. 1932-1947. Histoire du Cardinal de Richelieu. 6 vols. Paris.
Harrison, W. 1878. The Description of England in Shakespeare's Youth, edited by F. J. Furnivall. 3 vols. in 2. 1878, 1881. London.
Hart, Henry H. 1962. Luis de Camoëns and the Epic of the Lusiads. Stillwater, Okla.
Hartung, Fritz. 1910. Karl V. und die deutschen Reichsstände von 1546-1555. Historische Studien 1.
———. 1911. Die Wahlkapitulationen der deutschen Kaiser und Könige. Historische Zeitschrift 107: 306-44. Reprint U.S.A. 1968.
———. and Mousnier, Roland, 1955. Problèmes concernant la monarchie absolue. Relazioni del X Congresso internazionale di Scienze storiche. Florence.
———. 1950. Deutsche Verfassungsgeschichte, vom 15. Jahrhundert bis zur Gegenwart. 5th ed. Stuttgart.
Hay, Denys, ed. and trans. 1950. The Anglica Historia of Polydore Vergil, A.D. 1485-1537. London.
———. 1952. Polydore Vergil, Renaissance Historian and Man of Letters. Oxford.
———. 1960. Italy and Barbarian Europe. Italian Renaissance Studies, pp. 48-68.
Hayes, Carlton Joseph Huntley. 1931. The Historical Evolution of Modern Nationalism. New York.
———. 1960. Nationalism: A Religion. New York.
———. 1966. Essays on Nationalism. 3d ed. New York.
Heimpel, H. 1941. Hauptstädte Grossdeutschlands. Deutsches Mittelalter, pp. 154-70. Leipzig.
Herding, Otto. 1965. Jakob Wimpfeling, "Adolescentia." Munich.
Hertz, Friedrich O. 1937. Nationalgeist und Politik. Zurich.
———. 1956. Nationality in History and Politics. A Psychology and Sociology of National Sentiment and Nationalism. London.
———. 1957. The Development of the German Public Mind: A Social History of German

Political Sentiments, Aspirations, and Ideas. London.
Hettich, Ernest L. 1933. *A Study in Ancient Nationalism. The Testimony of Euripides.* Williamsport.
Historische Kommission bei der Bayerischen Akademie der Wissenschaften. 1962. *Deutsche Reichtagsakten unter Karl V.* 8 vols. 2d ed. (Vol. 1 edited by August Kluckhohn.) Göttingen.
——. 1972. Ibid., edited by Ernst Bock. 3 vols. Göttingen.
Hitier, M. J. 1903. La Doctrine de l'absolutisme. *Annales de l'Université de Grenoble* 15: 37-137, 417-532.
Hobsbawm, E. J. 1967. *The Age of Revolution.* Cleveland- New York.
Hoby, T. 1928. *The Book of The Courtier by Count Baldass. Castiglione done into English by Sir Th. Hoby, anno 1561.* London-Toronto-New York.
Hooper, Johan. 1843. *Early Writings,* edited by S. Carr, Parker Society vol. 11. Cambridge, Eng.
Hortleder, Friedrich. 1618. *Der römische Kaiser und königliche Majestät, auch des Heiligen Römischen Reichs Grafen . . . Handlungen . . . von 1546-1558.* 3 fol. vols. Leipzig.
Hotman, Francois. 1972. *Francogallia,* edited by R. Giesey, translated by J. H. M. Salmon. Cambridge, Eng.
Hugelmann, K. G. 1931. Das deutsche Nationalbewusstsein und der deutsche Nationalstaat im Mittelalter. *Historisches Jahrbuch* 51: 1-29, 445-84.
Hühns, Eric. 1958. 'Nationale' Propaganda im Schmalkaldischen Krieg. *Zeitschrift für Geschichtswissenschaft* 5: 1027-48.
Huizinga, J. 1943. *Im Bann der Geschichte,* translated by W. Kaegi. 2d ed. Basel.
Huppert, George. 1965. The Trojan Franks and their Critics. *Studies in the Renaissance* 12: 227-41.
Hurstfield, Joel, ed. 1966. *The Reformation Crisis.* New York.
Hutten, Ulrich von. 1859-1869. *Schriften,* ed. by Ed. Böcking. 7 vols. Leipzig.

I

Ilardi, Vincent. 1956. 'Italianità' among Some Italian Intellectuals in the Early 16th Century. *Traditio* 12: 339-67.
Irenicus, Franz. 1518. *Germaniae exegeseos volumina 12. Urbis Norinbergae descriptio Conrado Celte enarratore.* Nuremberg.

J

Jansen, Max. 1910. *Jacob Fugger, der Reiche, Studien und Quellen.* Leipzig.

Janssen, Johann. 1863-1872. *Frankfurts Reichskorrespondenz 1376-1519.* 2 vols. Freiburg.
Jayne, K. G. 1910. *Vasco da Gama and his Successors, 1460-1580.* London.
Joachimsen, Paul. 1910. *Geschichtsauffassung und Geschichtsschreibung in Deutschland unter dem Einfluss des Humanismus.* Leipzig.
——. 1921. *Der deutsche Staatsgedanke von seinen Anfängen bis auf Leibnitz und Friedrich den Grossen.* Munich.
——. 1970. *Gesammelte Aufsätze zu Renaissance, Humanismus und Reformation.* Aalen.
Johannet, René. 1923. *Le Principe des nationalités.* Paris.
Jung, Marc-René. 1966. *Hercule dans la littérature française du XVIe siècle.* Travaux d'Humanisme et Renaissance, vol. 79. Geneva.

K

Kaiser, G. 1961. *Pietismus und Patriotismus im literarischen Deutschland. Ein Beitrag zur Säkularisation.* Veröffentlichungen des Instituts für europäische Geschichte. Wiesbaden.
Kamen, Henry. 1965. *The Spanish Inquisition.* London.
Kelley, D. R. 1970. Murd'rous Machiavelli in France. *Political Science Quarterly* 85: 545-59.
Kermode, F. and Hollander, J. 1973. *The Oxford Anthology of English Literature.* 2 vols. Oxford.
Kern, Fritz. 1910. *Die Anfänge der französischen Ausdehnungspolitik bis zum Jahre 1303.* Tübingen.
Kirn, Paul. 1943. *Aus der Frühzeit des Nationalgefühls.* Leipzig.
——. 1944. *Politische Geschichte der deutschen Grenzen.* 3d ed. Leipzig.
Kisch, Guido. 1943. Nationalism and Race in Medieval Law. *The Jurist* 1: 48-73. (Extraordinary annual no. "Seminar".) Washington D. C.
Klein, Hans Wilhelm. 1957. *Latein und Volgare in Italien. Ein Beitrag zur Geschichte der italienischen National sprache.* Münchener Romanistische Arbeiten, vol. 12. Munich.
Kleinheyer, Gerd. 1968. *Die kaiserlichen Wahlkapitulationen: Geschichte, Wesen und Funktion.* Karlsruhe.
Knepper, Joseph. 1898. *Nationaler Gedanke und Kaiseridee bei den elsässischen Humanisten.* Erläuterungen zu Janssens Geschichte des deutschen Volkes, edited by L. Pastor. Freiburg.
Koebner, Richard. 1953. 'The Imperial Crown of this Realm': Henry VIII, Constantine the Great, and Polydore

116 | BIBLIOGRAPHY

Vergil. *London University Bulletin of the Institute of Historical Research* 26: 29-52.

Koenigsberger, H. G. 1969. *The Practice of Empire*. Ithaca.

———. 1975. Spain. In *National Consciousness, History, and Political Culture in Early-Modern Europe*, pp. 144-72, edited by Orest Ranum. Baltimore-London.

Kohn, Hans. 1939. The Nature of Nationalism. *American Political Science Review* 33: 1001-21.

———. 1948. *The Idea of Nationalism. A Study of its Origins and Background*. New York.

———. 1955. *Nationalism*. Princeton.

———. 1971. Soviet Communism and Nationalism. In *Soviet Nationality Problems*, edited by Edward Allworth, pp. 43-71.

Koht, Haldran. 1946-47. The Dawn of Nationalism in Europe. *American Historical Review* 52: 265-80.

Koppelmann, H. L. 1956. *Nation, Sprache und Nationalismus*. Leiden.

Kranz, Albert. [1548]. 1893. *Saxonia*, edited by P. Schaerffenberg. Meiningen.

Kristeller, P. O. 1965. *Renaissance Thought II. Papers on Humanism and the Arts*. New York.

Kukenheim, Louis. 1932. *Contributions à l'histoire de la grammaire italienne, espagnole et francaise à l'époque de la Renaissance*. Amsterdam.

Kurth, Godefroid. 1893. *Histoire poétique des Mérovingiens*. Paris.

———. 1919. *Etudes franques*. 2 vols. Paris-Brussels.

L

La Garanderie, Marie-Madeleine de, trans. and ed. 1967. *La Correspondance d'Erasme et de Guillaume Budé*. Paris.

Lando, Ortensio. 1548. *Commentario delle più notabili et mostruose cose d'Italia*. Venice.

Langosch, Karl, ed. and trans. 1962. *Enea Silvio Piccolomini, Deutschland*. Graz.

La Noue, Francois. 1967. *Discours politiques et militaires*, edited by F. E. Sutcliffe. Geneva-Paris.

Lapeyre, Henri. 1967. *Les Monarchies européennes du XVIe siècle. Les Relations internationales*. Nouvelle Clio. 31. Paris.

La Popelinière, Henri de. 1585. *L'Amiral de France et par occasion de celuy des autres nations*. Paris.

Latimer, Hugh, Bishop of Worcester. 1844. *Sermons and Remains*. Parker Society, vol. 16. Cambridge, Eng.

———. 1855. *Sermons*. Parker Society, vol. 20. Cambridge, Eng.

Lefebvre, G. 1935. French Nationalism. *Annales historiques de la Révolution Française* 12: 259-61.

Lefèvre de la Boderie, Guy. 1578. *La Galliade*

ou *de la révolution des arts et des sciences*. Paris.

Lefranc, A. 1893. *Histoire du Collège de France*. Paris.

Le Gentil, Georges. 1954. *Camoëns*. Paris.

Le Goff, J. 1964. La Conception francaise de l'université à l'époque de la Renaissance. In *Etudes et Documents: Institut d'histoire de la Faculté des lettres de Genève. Actes du Colloque international à l'occasion du VIe centenaire de l'Université Jagelonne de Cracovie*. Geneva.

Lemberg, Eugen. 1964. *Nationalismus*. 2 vols. Reinbeck bei Hamburg.

Léonard, Frédéric. 1693. *Recueil des traitez de paix, de trèves, de neutralité . . . par les rois de France avec tous les princes . . . de l'Europe . . . depuis près de trois siècles*. 6 vols. Paris.

Levine, Mortimer. 1962. A Parliamentary Title to the Crown in Tudor England. *Huntington Library Quarterly* 25: 121-27.

———. 1966. *The Early Elizabethan Succession Questions*. Stanford.

———. 1973. *Tudor Dynastic Problems, 1460-1571*. London-New York.

Levy, F. J. 1964. The Making of Camden's *Britannia. Bibliothèque d'Humanisme et Renaissance* 26: 70-97.

———. 1967. *Tudor Historical Thought*. Huntington Library, San Marino, Ca.

Lewis, C. S. 1954. *Oxford History of English Literature, excluding Drama*. Oxford.

Lewis, Lionel S. 1954. *St. Joseph of Arimathea at Glastonbury, or the Apostolic Church of Britain*. London.

Lewy, Guenter. 1960. *Constitutionalism and Statecraft during the Golden Age of Spain: A Study of the Political Thought of Juan de Mariana*. Travaux d'Humanisme et Renaissance, vol. 36

Lhotsky, A. 1944. "Apis Colonna," *Fabeln und Theorien über die Abkunft der Habsburger*. Institut für Geschichtsforschung und Archivwissenschaft in Wien, Mitteilungen. Innsbruck.

———. 1963. Die genealogischen Sammler im Dienst Maximilian I. *Mitteilungen des Instituts für österreichische Geschichtsforschung, Ergänzungsband 19. Quellenkunde zur mittelalterlichen Geschichte Österreichs*, pp. 443-56. Graz-Cologne.

———. 1968. Das Zeitalter des Hauses Österreich, 1520-1527. *Österreichische Akademie der Wissenschaften. Veröffentlichungen der Kommission für Geschichte Österreichs*. Reprint 1971. Vienna-Cologne-Graz Graz-Böhlau.

———. 1971. *Das Zeitalter des Hauses Österreich. Die ersten Jahre der Regierung Ferdinand I. in Österreich (1520-1527)*. (Collected essays from 1968, posthumously edited.) Vienna-Cologne-Graz-Böhlau.

Liebmann, Hans. 1910. *Deutschlands Land und Volk nach italienischen Bericht-*

erstattern der Reformationszeit. Historische Studien, vol. 81. Berlin.

Liliencron, Rochus von. 1869. *Die historischen Volkslieder der Deutschen.* 4 vols. Brunswick. Reprint 1966 Hildesheim.

Lintzel, Martin. 1961. *Ausgewählte Schriften. Zur Karolinger- und Ottonenzeit.* 2 vols. Berlin.

Livermore, H. L. 1947. *A History of Portugal.* Cambridge, Eng.

Livermore, H. V. 1966. *A New History of Portugal.* Cambridge, Eng.

Loades, D. M. 1965. *Two Tudor Conspiracies.* Cambridge, Eng.

———. 1965. The Enforcement of Reaction, 1553-1558. *Journal of Ecclesiastical History* 16: 54-66.

———. 1970. *The Oxford Martyrs.* New York.

———. 1974. *Politics and the Nation, 1450-1660. Obedience, Resistance and Public Order.* Brighton-Sussex.

Looz-Corswarem, Otto von. 1931. *Juan Ginés de Sepúlveda,* Göttingen.

Louis XIV. 1806. *Oeuvres de Louis XIV.* edited by Groinvelle and Grimard. 6 vols. Paris.

Luther, Martin. 1909. Sendbrief vom Dolmetschen (1530). In *Werke,* vol. 30, pp. 627-46. Weimar.

Lutz, Heinrich. 1964. *Christianitas afflicta. Europa, das Reich und die päpstliche Politik im Niedergang der Hegemonie Kaiser Karls V.: 1552-1556.* Göttingen.

———. 1968. Kaiser Karl V., Frankreich und das Reich. In *Frankreich und das Reich im 16. und 17. Jahrhundert.* Lectures by H. Lutz, F. H. Schubert, H. Weber. Göttingen.

Lyly, John. 1964. *Euphues: The Anatomy of Wit. Euphues and his England,* edited by M. W. Croll and H. Clemons. (First printed 1916). New York.

Lynch, J. 1961. Philip II and the Papacy. *Transactions of the Royal Historical Society* 11 (5th ser.): 23-42.

M

MacFarlane, I. D. 1959. Jean Salmon Maerin (1490-1550). *Bibliothèque d'Humanisme et Renaissance* 21: 55-84, 311-49.

Machiavelli, Niccolò. 1961-1968. *Opere.* Biblioteca di classici italiani. 8 vols. Milan.

———. 1961. *Lettere,* edited by Franco Gaeta. Milan.

Major, J. R. 1969. "The Renaissance Monarchy as Seen by Erasmus, More, Seyssel, and Machiavelli." In *Action and Conviction. Essays in Memory of E. H. Harbison.* pp. 17-31. Princeton.

Mango, Franco, ed. 1886. *Scelta di curiosità letterarie,* vol. 218. Bologna.

Mariana, Juan de. 1839-1840. *Historia general de España.* 10 vols. Barcelona.

Marillac, Charles de. 1885. *Correspondance politique de MM. de Castillon et de Marillac, 1537-1542.* Paris.

Martin, Victor. 1939. *Les Origines du gallicanisme.* 2 vols. Paris.

Martins, J. P. O. 1894. *Historia de Portugal.* 2 vols. in 1. Lisbon.

Matter, Hans. 1922. *Englische Gründungssagen von Geoffrey of Monmouth bis zur Renaissance. Ein Versuch.* Anglistische Forschungen, vol. 58. Heidelberg.

Mattingly, Garrett. 1959. *The Armada.* Boston.
———. 1964. *Renaissance Diplomacy.* Baltimore.

Maxwell-Stuart, (Mrs.). 1905. *The Tragedy of Fortheringhay.* London.

McKisack, May. 1971. *Medieval History in the Tudor Age.* Oxford.

Meier, Harri. 1935. Spanische Sprachbetrachtungen und Geschichtsschreibung am Ende des 15. Jahrhunderts. *Romanische Forschungen* 49: 1-20.

Meinecke, Friedrich 1927. Weltbürgertum und Nationalgeist. In *Werke,* vol. 5, edited by Hertzfield. Munich. Reprint ed. 1962, from 7th ed.

———. 1959. *Die Entstehung des Historismus,* edited by C. Hinrichs. Munich.

Meriam, Charles E. 1950. *Political Power.* Urbana.

Mesnard, Pierre. 1969. *L'Essor de la philosophie politique au XVIe siècle.* 3d ed. Paris.

Meyers Neues Lexikon. 1963. 8 vols. Leipzig

Misch, G. 1930. Die Stilisierung des eigenen Lebens in dem Ruhmeswerk Kaiser Maximilians, des letzten Ritters. *Nachrichten der Gesellschaft der Wissenschaften* Göttingen, pp. 435-59.

Mitscherlich, Waldemar. 1929. *Nationalismus. Die Geschichte einer Idee.* 2d ed. Leipzig.

Mitteis, Heinrich. 1959. *Der Staat des hohen Mittelalters.* 6th ed. Weimar.

Molfese, Franco. 1964. *Storia del brigantaggio dopo l'unità.* Milan.

Mombauer, Hans. 1936. Bismarcks Realpolitik als Ausdruck seiner Weltanschauung. *Historische Studien* 291. Reprint. Vaduz 1965.

Mommsen, Theodor. 1874-1875. *Römische Geschichte.* 3 vols. 6th ed. Berlin.

Mommsen, Wilhelm. 1939. Zur Beurteilung des Absolutismus. *Historische Zeitschrift* 158: 52-76.

Mönch, Walter. 1936. *Die italienische Platorenaissance und ihre Bedeutung für Frankreichs Literatur und Geistesgeschichte, 1450-1550.* Romanische Studien, vol. 40. Berlin.

Monod, Bernard. 1905. *Le Moine Guibert et son temps, 1053-1124.* Paris.

Monod, Gabriel. 1895-1897. Du rôle de l'opposition des races et des nationalités

dans la dissolution de l'empire carolingien.
*Annuaire de l'Ecole pratique des hautes
études 1896.* pp. 5-17. Paris.
Montaigne. 1958. *Essais,* edited by Maurice
Rat. 3 vols. Paris.
Morales, Ambrosio de. 1586. *Quinze
discursos de Ambrosio de Morales . . .
sobrino del maestro Hernan Perez de
Oliva, natural de Cordua.* Cordova.
Morison, Samuel Eliot. 1971. *The European
Discovery of America. The Northern
Voyages, A. D. 500-1600.* New York-
Oxford.
Morley, Lord Henry Parker. 1971. *Triumphes
of Fraunces Petrarcke,* edited by D. D.
Carnicelli. (Translated c. 1553.)
Cambridge, Mass.
Morris, Christian. 1953. *Political Thought in
England: Tyndale to Hooker.* Oxford.
———. 1967. *The Tudors.* New York.
Moser, J. J. 1767. *Von dem römischen
Kayser, römischen König und denen
reichsvicarien . . . .* Frankfurt.
Mousnier, Roland. 1966. *Etat et Société
sous Francois Ier et pendant le
gouvernement personnel de Louis XIV.*
Cours de Sorbonne. Paris
Mozley, James Freder. 1940. *John Foxe and
His Book.* New York.
Mulcaster, Richard. 1582. *The First Part of
the Elementarie which entreateth cheefelie
of the right writing of our English tung
. . .* London. Reprint 1970.
Murarasu, D. 1928. *La Poësie néo-latine et la
renaissance des lettres antiques en France,
1500-1549.* Paris.
Mutio, Justinopolitano. 1572. *Selva Odorifera.*
Venice.

N

Neale, J. E. 1958. *England's Elizabeth.* Folger
Shakespeare Library. Lecture in Celebration
of the 400th Anniversary of Her Accession.
London.
Nebrija, Antonio de. 1946. *Gramatica
castellana,* edited by P. G. Romeo and
L. O. Muñoz. Madrid.
Nef. J. U. 1934-1935. The Progress of
Technology and the Growth of Large-
Scale Industry in Great Britain. *The
Economical Historical Review* 5: 3-24.
Reprint New York 1957.
New Cambridge Modern History. 1957-1970.
14 vols. Cambridge, Eng.

O

Ocampo, Florian de. 1791-1792. *Cronica
General de España . . .* 10 vols. Madrid.

Ocete, Antonio Marín. 1946. Nebrija y
Pedro Mártir de Angléria. *Instituto
Antonio Nebrija, Miscellanea Nebrija,*
pp. 161-74. Madrid.
Offler, H. S. 1956. Aspects of Government
in the Late Medieval Empire. *Europe in
the Late Middle Ages,* pp. 217-47.
Evanston.
Oldys, William. 1808-1811. *Harleian
Miscellany, or A Collection of Scarce,
Curious, and Entertaining Pamphlets*
(1744-1746). 12 vols. London.
Oliva, Hernán Perez de. 1528. *Historia de la
Invención de la Yndias,* edited by J. J.
Arrom. Reprint Bogota 1965.
Oliveira Martins, J. P. 1894. *Historia de
Portugal.* 2 vols. in 1. 5th ed. Lisbon.
Ollivier, Albert. 1954. *Saint-Just.* Paris.
Olmedo, Felix G. 1944. *Nebrija en
Salamanca, 1475-1513.* Madrid.
Olschki, Leonardo. 1919. *Die Litgratur der
Technik und der angewandten Wissen-
schaften vom Mittelalter bis zur
Renaissance,* vol. 1. Heidelberg.
———. 1922. *Bildung und Wissenschaft im
Zeitalter der Renaissance in Italien.*
Leipzig-Florence-Rome-Geneva.
Olsen, V. N. 1973. *John Foxe and the
Elizabethan Church.* Berkeley.

P

Packard, Sidney R. 1964. A Medievalist
Looks at the Renaissance. *Smith College
Studies in History* 44: 3-12.
*Paladinos de linguagem. Antologia
Portuguesa. See under* Campos 1922-1926.
Parker, Matthew. 1853. *Correspondence.*
Parker Society. Cambridge, Eng.
———. 1605. *De Antiquitate Britannicae
Ecclesiae* (1572). Hanover.
Parkman, Francis. 1897-1901. *Works.*
15 vols. Boston.
Parks, George Bruner. 1961. *Richard Hakluyt
and the English Voyages,* edited by James
A. Williamson. 2d ed. New York.
———. 1961a. The First Italianate Englishmen.
Studies in the Renaissance 8: 197-216.
Paruta Paolo. 1954. *Discorsi politici.* 2 vols.
Scrittori politici italiani, edited by Giorgio
Candeloro. Bologna.
Paschoud, François. 1967. *Roma Aeterna.
Etude sur le patriotisme romain à l'époque
des grandes invasions.* Institut suisse de
Rome. Rome.
Pasquier, Estienne. 1633. *Oeuvres.* 2 fol. vols.
Paris.
———. 1966. *Lettres historiques, 1556-1594,*
edited by D. Thickett. Geneva.
Passerin, Alexandre d'Entrèves. 1947.
Reflections on the History of Italy.
Inaugural lecture. Oxford.

Pastor, José Francisco. 1929. *Las apologías de la lengua castellana en el siglo de oro.* Madrid.

Paul, Ulrich. 1936. Studien zur Geschichte des deutschen Nationalbewusstseins im Zeitalter des Humanismus und der Reformation. *Historische Studien* 298: 5-135.

Pauli, Reinhold. 1862. Englands Verhältnis zu der deutschen Kaiserwahl des Jahres 1519. *Forschungen zur deutschen Geschichte* 1: 413-36. Göttingen.

Pavolini, A. 1941. *Spagna e Italia dal 1559-1631.* Florence.

Pedro, Dr. 1855. *Colección de documentos ineditos para la historia de España.* 26: 340-65. Madrid.

Peletier du Mans, Jacques. 1607. *L'Arithmétique de Jacques Peletier du Mans.* 3d ed. Geneva.

Percy, Eustache. 1966. *John Knox.* Richmond.

Peres, Damião and Cerdeira, Eleutério, eds. 1927-1938. *Historia de Portugal.* 8 vols. Barcelos.

Perez de Oliva, Fernán [Hernán]. 1586. *Las Obras del maestro Fernán Perez de Oliva,* edited by Ambrosio de Morales. Cordoba.

— — —. 1965. *Historia de la Invençión de la* Perion, Joachim. 1555. *Perionii Joachimi Dialogorum de linguae gallicae origine, eiusque cum graeca cognatione libri 4.* Paris.

Pettie, George. 1581. *The Civile Conversation of M. Steeven Guazzo.* Reprint New York 1967.

Pfandl, Ludwig. 1929. *Geschichte der spanischen Nationalliteratur in ihrer Blütezeit.* Freiburg. Reprint Hildesheim 1967.

Philippson, Martin. 1878. Philip II. und das Papsttum. *Historische Zeitschrift* 39: 419-57.

Picard, Jean. 1556. *Joannis Picardi De prisca celtopaedia libri 5.* Paris.

Piccolomini, Aeneas Silvius. 1962. *Deutschland. Der Brieftraktat an Martin Mayer und Jacob Wimpfelings Antworten und Einwendungen gegen Eneas Silvio,* translated by A. Schmidt. Die Geschichtsschreiber der deutschen Vorzeit, no. 104. Graz.

Picot, Georges. 1888. *Histoire des Etats-Généraux.* 5 vols. Paris. Reprint New York 1969.

Pieri, Piero. 1952. *Il Rinascimento e la crisi militare italiana.* Turin.

Piggot, Stuart. 1951. William Camden and the Britannia. *Proceedings of the British Academy* 37: 199-217.

Pineas, Rainer, 1968. *Thomas More and Tudor Polemics.* Bloomington, Ind.

Pithou, Pierre. 1594. *Les Libertez de l'Eglise gallicane.* Paris.

Pocock, Nicholas. 1870. *Records of the Reformation.* 2 vols. Oxford.

Pölnitz, Götz, Freiherr von. [1949-1951.] *Jakob Fugger.* 2 vols. Tübingen.

Ponet, John. 1942. *A Short Treatise of Politike Power* (1556), edited by W. S. Hudson, Chicago.

Post, Gainer. 1953. Two Notes on Nationalism in the Middle Ages. *Traditio* 9: 281-96.

— — —. 1954. "Blessed Lady Spain." Vincentius Hispanus and Spanish National Imperialism in the 13th Century. *Speculum* 29: 198-209.

Pulgar, Hernando. 1943. *Crónicas españolas,* edited by J. de Mata Carriazo. 2 vols. Madrid.

Q

Queiroz Veloso, J. M. de. 1933. *Historia de Portugal: Historia politica,* vol. 5, edited by D. Peres and E. Cerdiera, 8 vols. Barcelos 1927-1938.

Quinn, D. B. 1940. *The Voyages and Colonising Enterprises of Sir Humphrey Gilbert.* 2 vols. London.

— — — 1965. Exploration and the Expansion of Europe. In *Comité international des sciences historiques. 12e Congrès international des sciences historiques,* pp. 45-59. Vienna.

— — —. 1974. *England and the Discovery of America, 1481-1620.* New York.

R

Rabe, Horst. 1971. *Reichsbund und Interim. Die Verfassungs- und Religionspolitik Karls V. und der Reichstage von Augsburg, 1547-1548.* Vienna.

Raleigh, Walter Alexander. 1910. *The English Voyages of the Sixteenth Century.* Glasgow.

Rankins, William. 1595. *The English Ape.* London.

Ranum, Orest, ed. 1975. *National Consciousness, History, and Political Culture in Early-Modern Europe.* Baltimore.

Rassow, P. 1932. *Die Kaiseridee Karls V., dargestellt an der Politik der Jahre 1528-1540.* Historische Studien, vol. 217. Berlin.

Ravencroft, W. 1928. The Coming of S. Joseph of Arimathias to England and the Way by which he came. *Milford-on-Sea Record Society* 4 (no. 3): 21-37.

Rebello da Silva, Luis Augusto. 1864. *Invasion et occupation du royaume de Portugal en 1580.* Paris.

Reeves, Marjorie. 1961. Joachimist Influences on the Idea of Last World Emperor.

Traditio 17: 323-70.

Renaudet, Auguste. 1954. *Erasme et l'Italie.* Geneva.

Ridolfi, Roberto. 1967. *The Life of Francesco Guicciardini,* translated by Cecil Grayson. London.

Riess, Hedwig. 1934. *Motive des patriotischen Stolzes bei den deutschen Humanisten.* Dissertation. Berlin.

Ritter, Gerhard. 1950. *Die Neugestaltung Europas im 16. Jahrhundert.* Berlin.

———. 1966. *Das deutsche Problem. Grundfragen deutschen Staatslebens.* 2d ed. Munich.

Rivoire, J. A. 1950. *Le Patriotisme dans le théâtre sérieux de la révolution, 1789-1799.* Paris.

Romera-Navarro, M. 1929. La Defensa de la lengua española en el siglo XVI. *Bulletin hispanique* 31: 204-55.

Romier, Lucien. 1926. *Nation et civilisation.* Paris.

Ronsard, Pierre. 1887-1893. *Oeuvres,* edited by C. Marty-Laveaux. 6 vols. Paris.

Rörig, F. 1937. Ursache und Auswirkung des deutschen Partikularismus. *Recht und Staat in Geschichte und Gegenwart* 120: 3-42. Tübingen.

———. 1948. Geblütsrecht und freie Wahl in ihrer Auswirkung auf die deutsche Geschichte. *Abhandlungen der deutschen Akademie der Wissenschaften zu Berlin, philosophisch-historische Klasse* 6.

Rosales, Luis, and Vivanco, Luis Fel. 1940. *Antología y prologos de poesía heroica del imperio.* 2 vols. Barcelona.

Rothfels, Hans. 1952. Grundsätzliches zum Problem der Nationalität. *Historische Zeitschrift* 174: 339-58.

Rudé, Georges. 1971. *Paris and London in the 18th Century. Studies in Popular Protest.* New York.

Ryan, Lawrence V. 1963. *Roger Ascham.* Stanford-London.

Rye, William Benchley. 1865. *England as Seen by Foreigners in the Days of Elizabeth and James the First.* London. Reprint 1967. New York.

S

Sachs, Hans. 1966. *Werke,* edited by K. M. Schiller. 2 vols. Bibliothek deutscher Klassiker. Berlin-Weimar.

Sachsen, Moritz von. 1900-1904. *Politische Korrespondenz des Herzogs und Kurfürsten Moritz von Sachsen,* edited by E. Brandenburg. 2 vols. Leipzig.

Sadler, Ralph. 1809. *State Papers of Sir Ralph Sadler,* edited by A. Clifford. 3 vols. Edinburgh.

Salcedo y Ruiz, Angel. 1915-1917. *La*

literatura española. 4 vols. 2d ed. Madrid.

Sandoval, Prudencio. 1955-1956. *Historia de la vida y hechos del emperador Carlos V.* 3 vols. Madrid.

Sanford, Charles L. 1961. *The Quest for Paradise. Europe and the American Moral Imagination.* Urbana.

Sañudo, Marin. 1873. *La Spedizione di Carlo VIII in Italia,* edited by R. Fulin. Venice.

Saulnier, V.-L. 1951. *Paris devant la renaissance des lettres.* Paris.

Scarisbrick, J. J. 1968. *Henry VIII.* Los Angeles.

Schaerffenberg, Paul, ed. 1893. *Die Saxonia des Albert Krantz.* Meiningen.

Schardius. 1673. *Germanicarum rerum.* 4 vols. Giessen.

Schneider, Reinhold. 1930. *Das Leiden des Camões, oder Untergang und Vollendung der portugiesischen Macht.* Hellerau.

Schottenloher, K. 1922. *Flugblatt und Zeitung.* Bibliothek für Kunst- und Antiquitätensammler, vol. 21. Berlin.

Schramm, Percy E. 1960. *Der König von Frankreich. Das Wesen der Monarchie vom 9. zum 16. Jahrhundert.* 2 vols. Weimar.

Schröcker, Alfred. 1950. *Maximilian I. Auffassung vom Königstum und das ständische Reich. Quellen und Forschungen aus italienischen Archiven und Bibliotheken* 50: 181-204. Tübingen.

Schubert, Friedrich Hermann. 1966. *Die deutschen Reichstage in der Staatslehre der frühen Neuzeit.* Schriften der historischen Kommission bei der Bayerischen Akademie der Wissenschaften, vol 7. Göttingen.

———. 1968. Französische Staatstheorie. In *Frankreich und das Reich im 16. und 17. Jahrhundert.* Lectures by H. Lutz, F. H. Schubert, and H. Weber. Göttingen.

Schulte, A. 1933. *Der deutsche Staat. Verfassung, Macht und Grenzen 919-1914.* Stuttgart-Berlin.

———. 1936. Anläufe zu einer festeren Residenz der deutschen Könige im Hochmittelalter. *Historisches Jahrbuch* 55: 131-42.

Seaver, Henry Latimer. 1928. *The Great Revolt in Castile. A Study of the Comunero Movement of 1520-1521.* Boston-New York.

Secret, Francois. 1969. *L'Esotérisme de Guy Le Fèvre de La Boderie.* Geneva.

Seguin, J.-P. 1961. *L'Information en France de Louis XII à Henri II.* Geneva.

Seton-Watson, Hugh. 1967. Nationalism and Imperialism. In *The Impact of the Russian Revolution 1917-1967. The Influence of Bolshevism on the World outside Russia,* pp. 134-206. Introduction by A. J. Toynbee. London-New York-Toronto.

Shafer, B. C. 1938. Bourgeois Nationalism in the Pamphlets on the Eve of the Revolution. *Journal of Modern History* 10: 31-50.

Schafer, B. C. 1955. *Nationalism: Myth and Reality*. New York.

Sicroff, A. S. 1960. *Les Controverses des statuts de "pureté de sang" en Espagne du XVe au XVIIe siècle*. Etudes de littérature étrangère et comparée, vol. 39. Paris.

Siebert, Frederic Seaton. 1952. *Freedom of the Press in England 1476-1776. The Rise and Decline of Government Controls*. Urbana.

Sigonio, Carlo. 1737. *Caroli Sigonii opera omnia. 6 vols*. Milan.

Silva Rego, A. da. 1965. *Portuguese Colonisation in the 16th Century: A Study of the Royal Ordinances (Regimentos)*. Johannesburg.

Simar, T. 1911. *Christophe de Longueil, humaniste (1488-1525)*. Université de Louvain, Recueil de travaux, vol. 31, ser. 1. Louvain.

Simone, Franco. 1949. *La Coscienza della Rinascità negli umanisti francesi*. Rome.

———. 1961. *Il Rinascimento francese. Studi e ricerche*. Turin.

Sleidan, Johannes. 1556. *Commentatorium de statu religionis et republicae Carolo Quinto Caesare libri 26*. Strassburg.

———. 1879. *Zwei Reden an Kaiser und Reich* (Strassburg 1544), edited by E. Böhmer. Tübingen.

Smith, Anthony D. 1971. *Theories of Nationalism*. London-Southampton.

Smith, D. Mack, ed. 1966. Risorgimento. In *The New Cambridge Modern History*, vol. 10, ch. 21. Cambridge, Eng.

Smith, G. Gregory. 1904. *Elizabethan Critical Essays*. 2 vols. Oxford.

Smith, H. Maynard. 1862. *Henry VIII and the Reformation*. New York.

Snyder, Louis L. 1968. *The New Nationalism*. Ithaca.

Soboul, Albert. 1960. La France à la veille de la révolution: Aspects économiques et sociaux. *Cours de Sorbonne*. Paris.

———. 1969. La France à la veille de la révolution: Les mouvements des idées. Ibid. Paris.

Spalatin, Georg. 1851. *Friedrich des Weisen Leben und Zeitgeschichte*. Jena.

Spitzer, Leo. 1954. The Problem of Latin Renaissance Poetry. *Studies in the Renaissance* 2: 118-38.

Starn, Randolph. 1968. *Donato Giannotti and His Epistolae*. Travaux d'Humanisme et Renaissance, vol. 97. Geneva.

Stella, Aldo. 1965. Utopie e velleità insurrezionali dei filoprotestanti italiani (1545-1547). *Bibliothèque d'Humanisme et Renaissance* 27: 133-82.

Storck, Wilhelm. 1897. *Vida e obras de Luis de Camões*. Translation of the 1st pt. of the German work by C. M. de Vasconcellos. Lisbon.

Strauss, David Friedrich. 1914. *Ulrich von Hutten*. Leipzig.

Strauss, Gerald. 1959. *Sixteenth Century Germany: Its Topography and Topographers*. Madison.

———. 1963. *Historian in an Age of Crisis: The Life and Work of Johan Aventinus 1477-1534*. Cambridge, Mass.

Strype, J. 1824. *Annals of the Reformation and Establishment of Religious and Other Various Occurrences in the Church of England during Queen Elizabeth's Happy Reign . . . .* 4 vols. Oxford. Reprint New York 1968.

Sudhoff, K. 1936. *Paracelsus. Ein deutsches Lebensbild aus den Tagen der Renaissance*. Leipzig.

Summerson, John. 1970. *Architecture in Britain 1530-1831*. The Pelican History of Art. Baltimore.

Switzer, Rebecca. 1927. *The Ciceronian Style in Fr. Luis de Granada*. New York.

Syme, Ronald. 1939. *The Roman Revolution*. Oxford.

T

Taylor, F. L. 1921. *The Art of War in Italy, 1494-1529*. Cambridge, Eng.

Thou, A. de. 1625. *Thuani Historiarum sui temporis ab anno 1543 usque ad annum 1607*. 138 bks. in 7 vols. Frankfurt.

———. 1742. *Histoire universelle*. 11 vols. Basel.

Ticknor, George. 1965. *History of Spanish Literature*. 3 vols. 6th ed. New York.

Tiedemann, Hans. [1913]. *Tacitus und der Nationalbegriff der deutschen Humanisten Ende des 15. und Anfang des 16. Jahrhunderts*. Berlin.

Thomas, William. 1861. *The Pilgrim*. Notes by J. A. Froude. London.

Tocco, Vittorio de. 1924. Un progetto di confederazione italiana nella seconda metà del Cinquecento. *Archivo storico italiano*, vol 1 (ser. 7). Florence.

———. 1926. *Ideali d'independenza in Italia durante la preponderanza spagnuola*. Messina.

Toynbee, A. J. ed. 1962. *Greek Historical Thought*. New York.

Treitschke, Heinrich von. 1886. *Historische und politische Aufsätze*. 2 vols. 5th ed. Leipzig.

Trevor-Roper, H. 1971. *Queen Elizabeth's First Historian, William Camden and the Beginning of English 'Civil History.'* Neale Lecture in English History. London.

U

Ullmann, Walter. 1949. The Development of the Medieval Idea of Sovereignty. *The*

English Historical Review 64: 1-33.

V

Valdès, Alfonso de. 1952. *Dialogue of Lactancio and an Archdeacon (1527),* trans. with introd. by J. E. Longhurst. New Mexico.
Valla, Lorenzo. 1544. *Laurentii Vallae de linguae latinae elegantia libri 6.* Paris.
Vaussard, M. ed. 1924. *Enquête sur le nationalisme.* Paris.
Veniero, Domenico. 1751. *Rime,* edited by P. A. Serassi. Bergamo.
Vettori, Francesco. 1848. *Sommario della storia d'Italia, 1511-1527.* Archivio italiano, vol. 6. Florence.
Vocht, Henry de. 1934. Damião de-Goes and his *Oratio postliminio ad universitatem.* In *Umanistica lovanensia. Texts and Studies about Louvain Humanists in the first half of the XVIth Century,* pp. 609-98. Louvain.
Voight, Georg. 1880. *Die Wiederbelebung des classischen Alterthums.* 2 vols. 2d ed. Berlin.
Voigt, Johann. 1852. *Markgraf Albrecht Alcibiades von Brandenburg-Kulmbach.* Berlin.

schaft für deutsche Sprache, vol. 1. Lüneburg.
Wiesflecker, Hermann. 1971. *Kaiser Maximilian I: Das Reich, Österreich und Europa an der Wende zur Neuzeit.* Munich.
Wilks, Michael. 1963. *The Problem of Sovereignty in the Later Middle Ages: The Papal Monarchy with Augustinus Triumphus and the Publicists.* Cambridge, Eng.
Wilson, Thomas. 1553. *The Arte of Rhetorique.* Introd. by R. H. Bowers. Gainesville 1967.
Wimpfeling, J. 1505. *Epitoma rerum germanicarum.* Strassburg.
——— 1885. *Germania,* translated by Ernst Martin. Strassburg.
Winterhagen, Jürg. 1934. *Die Vorstellung vom auserwählten Volk in England.* Dissertation. Berlin.
Woodward, E. L. 1916. *Christianity and Nationalism in the Later Roman Empire.* London.
Wright, L. B. 1943. *Religion and Empire: The Alliance between Piety and Commerce in English Expansions 1558-1625.* Reprint New York. 1965.
——— 1970. *Gold, Glory and the Gospel.* New York.

W

Waas, Glenn Elwood. 1966. *The Legendary Character of Kaiser Maximilian.* Reprint. New York.
Waddington, C. T. 1855. *Ramus, sa vie, ses écrits et ses opinions.* Paris.
Wagner, Georg. 1969. Maximilian I. und die politische Propaganda. In *Maximilian I. Ausstellungskatalog,* pp. 33-45. Innsbruck.
Wagner, Joachim. 1929. *Nationale Strömungen in Deutschland am Ausgang des Mittel-alters.* Werda.
Waldeck, O. 1910. Die Publizistik des Schmal-kaldischen Krieges. *Archiv für Reforma-tionsgeschichte* 7: 1-55.
——— 1911. Die Publizistik des Schmalkal-dischen Krieges (pt. 2). Ibid. 8: 44-133.
Walek-Czarnecki, T. 1928. Le Facteur national dans l'histoire ancienne. In *VIe Congrès international des sciences historiques,* pp. 559-61. Oslo.
Weill, Georges. 1938. *L'Europe du XIXe siècle et l'idée de nationalité.* Paris.
Weinberg, B. 1950. *Critical Prefaces of the French Renaissance.* Evanston.
Weisgerber, Joahnn. [1948]. *Die Entdeckung der Muttersprachen.* Schriften der Gesell-

Y

Yardeni, Myriam. 1966. Antagonismes nationaux et propagande durant les guerres de religion. *Revue d'Histoire moderne et contemporaine* 13: 273-84.
——— 1971. *La Conscience nationale en France pendant les guerres de religion (1559-1598).* Louvain-Paris.
Yates, Frances A. 1947. *The French Academies of the 16th Century.* Studies of the Warburg Institute, no. 15. London. Reprint New York 1968.

Z

Zeeveld, W. Gordon. 1948. *Foundation of Tudor Politics.* London-New York.
Zeller, G. 1934. Les Rois de France candidats à l'Empire. *Revue Historique* 173: 273-311, 497-534.
Zeumer, K. 1913. *Quellensammlung zur deutschen Reichsverfassung in Mittel-alter und Neuzeit.* 2 vols. 2d ed. Tübingen.

Index

Not included in the Index are names that occur solely either in the two lists following the Introduction or in the alphabetically ordered section of the Italian chapter. References to footnotes are in italics.

A

Acton, Lord, *90*
Aeneas Silvius Piccolomini, 45, 97
Alba, 47
Alberti, F. L., *93*
Alcalà, 61, *101*
Alcibiades, Albrecht, 51, 52, 53, *99*
Algiers, 26
Alps, 37, 71, *94*
Alsatia, 45
America, 27, 80, *107-108*
Americanization, 65
Ammirato, Scipio, *93*
Amyot, J., 67-68
antiquaries. *See* origins
Arco, R. del, *91*
Ariosto, 27, 33, 38-39
Armada, 26, 82
Aroaz, A., 23-24
Arthur (legendary king of England), 76, *105*
Ascham, R., 50, 85, *99, 108*
Astraîn, A., 23
astrology, *104*
Aylmer, J., 79, 80-81

B

Bale, J., 75-76
Barrès, M., 58
Bataillon, M., 25, *91*
Beau, A. F., *91*
Bebel, H., 46
Belleforest, F., 68
Biblical ancestry. *See* origins
Bismarck, O. von, 6
Blignières, A. de, 67
Bloch, M., 14, *100*
Boas, G., *89*
Bodin, J., 63-64, *99*
Boehmer, H., 25
Boleyn, Anne, *105*
Bourdon, A., *90*
Brennus, 76
Bruni, L., *93*
Brunot, F., 67
Brutus, 76, *105*
Budé, G., 60-62, *96, 97, 100, 101, 102*

Burghley, Lord, 79, 81
Bush, D., *89*
Butterfield, H. *89, 90*

C

Caesar, Julius, 55, 64
Calais, 59
Camden, W., 81, 82, *108*
Camoẽs, L. de, 19
Capet, Hugh, 65
Carpio, B. de, 27
Castiglione (*Il Cortigiano*), 33, 57, 83, *100*
Cateau-Cambrésis, Treaty of, 30
Catherine of Medici, 60
Catholicism, 7-8, 74, 77, *106*
Celtis, C., 45, 55, 56
Celts, 55, 63, 64, 65
Cervantes, 26, *92*
Chabod, F., 5, *93, 94, 98*
characteristic of nations, 57-59, *100*
Chamard, H., 67, 69
Chambord, Treaty of, 51, 52, *98*
Champier, S., 60
Chanson de Roland, 27, 58
Chapuys, E., 76, *105*
Charlemagne, 43, 47
Charles V, 17, 21, 22, 27, 39, 43, 47, 48-50, 51-52, 57, *96, 102*
chauvinism, 3, 58
Chevalier, L., *90*
Chièvres, 47
Cobos (de los), 47
Collège de France, 61, *102*
Collège des lecteurs royaux, 61
Communism, 7-8
Connan, F., 63
Constantine, 76, 79, *105, 107*
Coquille, G., 65, *103*
Cromwell, T., 78
Croy, 47

D

Dante, 29, 40
Damião de Gois, 19, *91*
Davys, J., 80, *107*
Dolet, E., 67-68, *102, 103*